2/97

291.4 C

DATE DUE

3577
0851

BIO—
SPIRITUALITY

SECOND
EDITION

BIO—
SPIRITUALITY

FOCUSING
AS A WAY
TO GROW

PETER A. CAMPBELL, PH.D.

EDWIN M. MCMAHON, PH.D.

FOREWORD BY ROBERT T. SEARS, S.J.

 Loyola Press

Loyola Press
3441 North Ashland Avenue
Chicago, Illinois 60657

Cover and interior design by Anne Marie Mastandrea

Library of Congress Cataloging in Publication Data

Campbell, Peter A., 1935-
    Bio-spirituality: focusing as a way to grow / by Peter A. Campbell & Edwin M. McMahon. – 2nd ed.
        p.   cm.
    Includes bibliographical references.
    ISBN 0-8294-0937-8
    1. Spiritual life. I. McMahon, Edwin M.,1930-   .
II. Title.
BL624.C34   1997
291.4–dc21   96-39189
                                                            CIP

97 98 99 00 01 / 10 9 8 7 6 5 4 3 2 1

Contents

Foreword   vii

Preface to the 1997 revised   xvii
and expanded version

Introduction
"A lookout point in the universe"   xxiii

1   A leap into bodily knowing   1

2   Learning to focus
Practical steps toward the art of allowing   15

3   Why we teach Focusing
in the context of spirituality   51

4   Humor, playfulness, and surprise
The vulnerability of ego   63

5   Restoring inner process
The evolution of God consciousness   87

6 An ancient perspective
   The evolving body of spirit   103

7 The body's approach to death
   A story being born in every dying   117

8 Toward a new paradigm
   for Western spirituality   129

Appendix 1   An updated summary
             of Focusing steps
             (as we teach them)   139

Appendix 2   Process-Skipping: A block
             to the body-life of Spirit   177

Appendix 3   From whom should I learn
             Bio-Spiritual Focusing?   195

Appendix 4   Ten Learnings from Bio-
             Spirituality that draw us
             into a global spirituality   203

Notes   207

The Institute for Bio-Spiritual Research   211

Foreword

Changes in therapy and human experience raise questions for faith and theology. One such development is noted in Alexander Lowen's *Bioenergetics:* "The failure of verbal therapies to produce significant changes in personality," he writes, "is responsible for an increasing interest in non-verbal and body approaches" (p. 120). In this book, Campbell and McMahon argue persuasively that a similar shift of attention to the body's wisdom is needed today for Christian spirituality. Religion of the head has left us divided from one another and from ourselves. We need to get to deeper roots of the Spirit than formulated beliefs.

The authors have found Focusing, the therapeutic method developed by Eugene Gendlin of the University of Chicago, to be a way into the body's wisdom. At one level, focusing is a therapy that helps people resolve human conflicts and get in touch with their own inner direction. At a deeper level, which is the very core of this book, Focusing becomes a form of spiritual meditation that helps people find their own form of self-transcendence.

Meditation has taken many forms in world religions: from wordless, imageless centering of Zen Buddhism and Christian Zen, the mystical mantras of the Orient and the popular Jesus Prayer which developed within Eastern Orthodox Christianity, to the mandalas of Tibet, the icons of Orthodoxy, and the Ignatian contemplations on the mysteries of Jesus' life in Western Christianity. Each form draws a person to a transcendent cosmic truth beyond ordinary life, yet within it. Focusing has many similarities. It is a discipline of attending to the bodily felt sense of what is at work in one's life. This felt sense is more basic than words or images. However, when it touches the transcendent ground of our ongoing life, it yields fresh images and words that release life and energy formerly stifled by traditional consciousness. Thus Focusing, like traditional meditation, touches a deeper cosmic process, but it does so in a way that is unique to each individual in his or her own time and place. We each share this "cosmic process"—which the authors relate to the divine Spirit in the world—so that it can heal our isolation and fear and lead us to recognize our participation in a dynamic universal truth. If many were growing in this spiritual focusing, God's image would emerge ever more clearly in our world.

The process of Focusing, seen at that spiritual depth, gives the authors a fresh way of viewing Christian truth as well as the truth of other worldviews. Since one's felt sense is prior to specific beliefs or formulations, Focusing promises to unite persons of various persuasions, to heal wounds of misunderstanding and alienation, and to open people to sharing a common future unfolding in the world. It touches into a level of humanity united in a single evolving world, a "gifted" or "graced" unity that is not caused by efforts of the ego but rather by surrender to this common underlying process.

Yet we resist this unity for many reasons. Our ego structures, both individual and communal, often mask weakness and pain. Focusing makes one attend to areas of hurt and weakness lodged deep in the memories of the body, which forgets nothing. Conventional beliefs and orthodoxies often merely protect us from these vulnerable areas. We fight and make war to defend these beliefs, and it is a veritable "crucifixion" to face the insecurity of surrendering them. But further, our ego structures are "moral achievements." They discipline unbridled sexuality and aggression that our Western Christian culture sees lurking in our bodies. Our permissive generation is in reaction against such Victorian mores, but the same separation of body from spirit lies in both. Sexuality is alienated from responsible spirituality. The body's desires then get separated from their deeper awareness of "being unto death," and their deeper ground in God. As Ernest Becker pointed out in *The Denial of Death*, we flee death and escape into idealizations of sexual conquest and success. But the body knows the dying within, and only by facing it can we confront our true reality and our true spirituality. Focusing thus contacts our inner vulnerability and repressed pain, but that very contact releases new energy and fresh hope.

The courageous decision to face that inner truth is how Campbell and McMahon understand conversion and faith. That faith is grounded not in formulated beliefs but in the experience of the unfolding process itself. The very process of believing gives us an analogous way of understanding its deepest ground, the triune God. "I" focus on a "felt sense" which "unfolds" into who I am in the process of becoming. Analogously, the Father (I) forms his perfect Image (felt sense) which gives rise to an unfolding process of integration and self-transcendence (Holy Spirit). Focusing is a doorway beyond formulations of belief to faith or believing itself. As one moves more deeply into it, every event, every "felt-meaning," can become a religious event opening one to incarnate Spirit unfolding in evolution. Focusing does not *cause* this redemptive contact with Spirit. It opens the way. The transforming event itself is always perceived as gift—as grace—and a growing gratitude and reverence emerge in one who lives out this spiritual type of focusing.

The perspectives opened by spiritual focusing are exciting. Yet several questions will likely come to the Christian's mind that will need to be addressed before he or she can be fully receptive to this new view. For the Christian, Jesus is the unique mediator of relationship to the Father. How does his person appear as one opens to the cosmic process? Should not Christian meditation center on Jesus? Similarly, Jesus is the Second Person of the Trinity, not just an expression of the self-knowledge of the Father. And the Holy Spirit is "another Paraclete" *(John 14:16)*, another person in the triune God, not just a process of spiritual evolution. How do these personal characteristics appear in the focusing process? Further, do we not believe in doctrinal definitions that remain permanently true, such as the Son is of "like being" with the Father (Nicaea) and fully human (Chalcedon)? Are these truths preserved if one takes one's ground at a preverbal level? Or more specifically, can we fully trust our bodily wisdom when we have experienced how narrow desires or angers have led us away from God and others? How is one to discern between movements that are of God and those that are not? Surely not everything that transcends ordinary consciousness is of God.

These are serious questions that will need to be faced. Yet they do not have to be fully resolved before one enters fully into the process of spiritual focusing so well presented in this book. Focusing as a spiritual discipline has been a help to many who no doubt interpret their experience according to their own frame of reference. The theoretical questions do not have to be fully resolved before the reader can profit from the method of meditation presented here.

For Christians who want to pursue the theoretical questions more fully, the following observations may help. A first observation regards theological method. Every theologian or reflective Christian frames questions and understands according to his or her religious experience or conversion. An academician asks academic questions, a mystic mystical questions. The authors show that our bodies and their memories are key to authentic experience. Since how one interprets Scripture or tradition, God or Trinity, depends on what experience one appeals to as analogous, we will have to get beyond concepts to the underlying bodily experience if our interpretation is to be authentic. Focusing is an excellent way to this bodily experience.

Secondly, this means that the body is far more important than Western theology or spirituality has conceded. The negative attitude of Western Christianity toward the body is not biblical. The authors of Scripture saw the human person as embodied. It was the Greeks and the Fathers influenced by Greek philosophy who distinguished between body and spirit in a way that contributed to our modern separation of body and spirit. The evangelists believed in the resurrection of body, not just the immortality of the soul (a Greek notion), and they came to see this resurrection as already active in believers. That means that our bodily existence is already being transformed through the Spirit of Jesus' resurrection, and that the believer can touch this Spirit at the depth of inner experience and in the bond of love uniting believers.

Thirdly, however, a caution is needed. Is there such a thing as noninterpreted experience? Or is the interpretation or symbol that arises spontaneously from one's unconscious a final criterion of meaning? It seems already to be a theological option to believe in a universal unity of cosmic process grounding bodily awareness. One may believe, as Jung seems to have done following Kant, that one's experience of God is uniquely individual, and that a "common unity" would only reduce people to a low common denominator. Or regarding death, the body may, as the authors suggest, have intimations of existence beyond death, or it may lead others of a more existentialist bent to see death as a barrier to be faced with Stoic heroism. Does bodily experience move one decisively to either option? Is it not rather a prior faith or conversion that moves one to interpret bodily experience in one or the other way? What the authors present seems already to be based on a Christian option for universal salvation or an oriental view of the unity of all being. The basis of that option is not simply bodily awareness of spirit, as important as that may be. As Christians, the authors believe in the resurrected Lordship of Jesus and the Spirit as potentially universal. The Zen Buddhist or Hindu Advaitist believes in the nonduality of all experience as revealed through enlightenment. These basic conversions color each one's bodily awareness as well as being affected by that awareness. Ultimately everyone uses some norm to interpret experience, and experience in turn affects the understanding of the norm.

Finally, for the Christian that norm is the person and life-death-resurrection of Jesus Christ. What effect would this specifically Christian perspective have on spiritual focusing? What importance does Focusing then have? It would seem to be a very significant way of becoming aware of one's unique embodied being in the here and now in dialogue with the normative Spirit of Jesus' life. The Spiritual Exercises of St. Ignatius lead the exercitant into contemplations of the mysteries of Jesus' life, death, and resurrection and ask the person to "draw fruit," that is, to bring the Spirit of Jesus' life into dialogue with one's own life. Focusing seems ideally suited to complement such a process—to bring the uniqueness of one's own spiritual process into dialogue with Jesus' life. One's felt sense gives rise to an image or word that releases a shift of perspective or energy. For the Christian, the deepest meaning of this shift is that it transforms believers into the image of God revealed in the Spirit of Jesus' life. Thus, if one related one's experience to the scriptural portrait of Jesus, one would not only gain new insight into Jesus' life but also illumine and energize one's own life in a new way.

Without saying it, the authors have used a similar method of correlation by using Judeo-Christian Scripture to help illumine focusing, and by using focusing to open new meanings of Scripture. All I would add is the interpersonal dimension—the dialogue with the person and life of Jesus and the persons of the Trinity that is at the heart of Christian spirituality. Other religious traditions would find other meanings, but openness to experience as basic to dialogue would lead each tradition to respect the process of the others and thus lead to a pluralistic unity analogous to the cosmic unity envisioned in the book. Spiritual focusing would thus open each of us to the excitement of seeing our lives unfold in a common spirit, which the Christian would see as rooted in the one Spirit of Jesus who also reveals the Father's love. Focusing does not interpret itself, but it may well be an important key to unlock the mysteries of God's work in the depth of creation and in each individual, revealed in Jesus' life and Spirit and ever unfolding in human evolution.

Robert T. Sears, S.J.
Loyola University of Chicago

Preface to the 1997 revised and expanded version

When *Bio-Spirituality* first appeared in 1985 we never imagined it would become the spiritual classic that it is today, growing in demand rather than fading away. "Serious seekers" from diverse walks of life and religious traditions seem determined to learn more about the mystery of spirit unfolding within their own bodies.

Writing of Western society's desperate need for a more embodied spiritual discipline, Carl Jung noted almost forty years ago that:

No insight is gained . . . by imitating methods which have grown up under totally different psychological conditions. In the course of the centuries the West will produce its own yoga.[1]

Yoga is about the body and about the body's involvement in spiritual experience. If we lack a truly Western yoga, it is because we Westerners can talk about the body but we have failed to *incorporate* it into our spirituality. We don't know how to do that. This book remains in print twelve

years after it was first published because the people who read it recognize that it helps them to do
what they know they need to do. And, they then
tell other people who help spread the word!

The process of body awareness that we describe
in the following pages is called "Focusing." It was
developed by Dr. Eugene Gendlin at the
University of Chicago. Part of our book describes
the practical details and steps of how we teach
Focusing. We call our approach *Bio-Spiritual
Focusing* because we emphasize an openness to
the potential for connecting in a bodily way with
the "gift dimension of life," as well as with a spiritual "More" or "Transcendence" that is implicit
within the Focusing process. What began as a
purely therapeutic psychological tool has, in our
view, the potential to become a widespread and
accessible cross-cultural spiritual path for ordinary people as we enter the new millennium.

In this book we describe neglected and little
used information that has been buried within the
Judeo-Christian tradition. There are clues here
that can help both Christians and non-Christians
alike to better understand the process of their own
wholeness and ultimate identity *when the clues can
be approached through our body's ability to know, and
not just out of familiar patterns of rational thinking or
interpretation.*

In addition to a completely revised appendix
on the Steps of Focusing, this expanded version
adds several new areas that were not developed

in the earlier printing. First, there is a clear explanation why many techniques and so-called "New Age" methods fail to produce the much sought-after wisdom and experience that only mature when we allow "space for grace" in our body's awareness.

During recent years, there has been growing concern over the widespread emergence of violent religious fundamentalism across the globe. Simplistic religious solutions to complex social problems as well as the growing use of political power to impose these interpretations and solutions on everyone gives rise to apprehension. Today, more people want to understand the difference between religious practices that promote unity, peace, and community and those that easily become fanatical, deeply divisive, manipulative, and violent. In so many instances, the followers of religion seem pathologically addicted to the practices and outlooks that they so passionately espouse.

The process of Bio-Spiritual Focusing directly addresses this profound contemporary problem. Through his research, Dr. Gendlin has identified the *psychological* mechanism that locks addictive patterns in place and makes them so resistant to change, whether within an individual, a culture, or a social group such as organized religion. Gendlin calls this mechanism a *process-skipping structure*. We describe it in a new appendix that has been added to this version of *Bio-Spirituality*. Within this same appendix we outline five easily understood criteria to help our readers evaluate the health or potential process-skipping pathology in spiritual and growth practices. Bio-Spiritual Focusing offers a healthy path to wholeness by providing access to a gifting wisdom within our own body.

A second addition to this expanded version is new material drawn from our network's past decade of using Bio-Spiritual Focusing. This experience offers exciting hints about what lies ahead as we are drawn forward into the relatively unexplored potential that our body's consciousness contains for nurturing the birth of a global spirituality.

Beyond diverse doctrines, religious interpretations, language, ethnic, cultural, and social variations, the one reality that we all share in common with everyone else is the human organism! We may be divided by our ideas and interpretations, but we remain firmly united in the body-life of spirit itself. This is the ultimate common ground and foundation for lasting peace. Ten learnings from Bio-Spirituality that draw us into a global spirituality are summarized for the reader in an additional new appendix. Finally, useful suggestions for selecting a Focusing teacher or companion who is sensitive to the intrinsic spirituality of this process have been added at the end of the book.

Bio-Spiritual Focusing is about our journey toward healing and wholeness. It describes a simple, practical way to include your body's wisdom and knowing on this awesome journey.

Introduction

"A lookout point in the universe"

The year was 1799. A French soldier attached to an expeditionary force in Egypt was busy preparing fortifications for the Nile Delta town of Rashid—called Rosetta by the Europeans. Suddenly, during the course of his excavation he unearthed a slab from an ancient temple. It was made of black basalt, stood about a meter high, and contained what appeared to be the same inscription written in three different languages—Egyptian hieroglyphics, Demotic, and Greek.

Up to this point in time Egyptian hieroglyphics had remained indecipherable. They had resisted every attempt to crack the coded language that veiled hidden wonders within this most ancient civilization. Now, with the chance thrusting of a laborer's shovel the inscrutable barrier had been broken. By comparing the Greek letters for Ptolemy and Cleopatra with their hieroglyphic counterparts, a door was finally opened. The first ray of light in modern times fell across the dark interior of this long-silent culture. Scholars hovered in awe before the treasure that now lay at their fingertips. The Rosetta Stone was their key. It was a lookout point from which to peer into the soul of a vast, unspoken civilization.

The inward journey outlined in this book may be compared to the first steps in a venture that can lead not merely into the mysteries of another culture; it can be an opening forward as the human species prepares for the next phase of consciousness evolution itself!

Yet, there are still more parallels in this journey with the finding of the Rosetta Stone. There are significant clues about what lies ahead within human unfolding. A superb humanistic vision can light our way on this journey into ourselves. Much of the revelation about what it means to be human, however, lies coded within the wisdom tradition of world religions. There is a silent treasure there hidden beneath centuries of neglect and misinterpretation.

This book grew from searching, searching for a practical way to enter ordinary living so the meaning of being human and being uniquely oneself might lead each of us forward into the mystery of some larger Awareness. These pages will attempt to describe the ingredients of a lived spirituality that actually facilitates change. We are not concerned with change in the realm of religious *ideas*. Rather, we look toward a transformation that will support human wholeness as this can unfold within a greater organismic evolution—a growing cosmic congruence.

This is not, therefore, a collection of denominational religious teachings or truths. We describe, instead, a quality of human consciousness, a lifestyle wherein an awareness potential of *the body* is absolutely indispensable for spiritual knowing. We call this capacity for more integral presence *bio-spirituality*.

Once our entire consciousness is encouraged to open and mature, then the root of our biological connectedness to a vast Process of Unification can gradually reveal itself within our daily lives. There is an awareness within our bodies that leads beyond ourselves. A bio-consciousness. Bio-presence. It does not confine us to what we can figure out and control with our minds, but it turns, instead, toward *an openness* within bodily knowing.

Whether we choose to recognize it or not, each of us is an integral living cell within the evolution of some Larger Body Process. The maturation of this awareness, however, does not occur by reason of what we *do*, but by virtue of a wholeness we *allow* to break through inside ourselves. Unity within the human family, our planet, and some greater cosmic congruence matures inside the knowing that is proper to our bodies. It is not so much thinking as *resonance*. The tuning fork of evolution strikes an inviting chord within the organicity of ourselves.

In the pages that follow we would like to share the beginnings of a bio-spiritual treasure hunt. It is a journey that has drawn the two of us into a dramatic new perspective on the mysteries and revelation contained within our own religious tradition. Certain clues within the Judeo-Christian heritage have opened for us a challenging new way to look at the bio-spiritual implications of *human development itself!*

We believe a time has come in human history, if for no other reason than for the survival of life on our planet, when we must turn our energy and our priorities toward encouraging just such consciousness-potential. We need to find simple, practical ways to support this humanizing capability within millions of people so that an experience of planetary unity may be revealed.

People blocked from growth cannot assimilate the crucial, life-saving data that lies hidden beneath their narrow and limited perception. When personal meaning becomes unblocked, however, they can often be freed from the fear and defensiveness that so often lead to violence.

In this book we want to share with you, our reader, a mode of self-awareness that offers an exciting and significant step toward developing a bio-spirituality that responds to these critical needs. We describe what we feel are the key ingredients in a humanizing spirituality. These include psychological dynamics that transcend the teachings of any particular religion. Yet they are found in the wisdom literature and perennial philosophy of the world's great spiritual traditions. They are often arcane, enigmatic, and inaccessible to the average person; popular religion has rarely been able to utilize the wisdom that lies hidden within the venerable patrimonies of the past.

The religious experience of unity and wholeness lies rooted in a bio-spirituality deep within
the evolution of ourselves and of the cosmos itself.
The religions of the world must now step toward
this energizing experience on a massive popular
scale if they are to make a significant contribution
to the course of human history. Values, perceptions, and lifestyles must change radically or the
world's growing arsenal of nuclear weapons will
eventually destroy us.

Religion seems to be at a crossroads in our time.
Because of an exhausting preoccupation with
morality, it has generally failed to call forth any
depth of spiritual vision within its adherents.
"Doing good and avoiding evil" simply does not
provide the energetic stuff from which an evolutionary vision can be fashioned. Without breadth,
height, and depth—the fresh air of mountain
tops—religion tends to be small and niggardly.
There is an inevitable decline.

The priest and scientist Pierre Teilhard de
Chardin expressed the problem well:

In its present state Morality offers a painful
spectacle of confusion. Apart from a few elementary laws of individual justice, empiri-
cally established and blindly followed, who
can say what is good and what is evil? Can we
even maintain that Good and Evil exist while
the evolutionary course on which we are
embarked has no clear direction? Is striving

really a better thing than enjoyment, disinterest better than self-interest, kindness better than compulsion? Lacking a look-out point in the Universe, the most sharply opposed doctrines on these vital matters can be plausibly defended.[1]

"A look-out point in the universe." That's what we want to share in this book. Not some new doctrine or interpretation, but a way to stand in ourselves. A quality of experience. A point of spiritual resonance.

When Teilhard de Chardin wrote his reflections on morality in 1942, he lamented that the best way of reaching the desired lookout point had yet to be found. In this book we want to describe what we regard as an important *step* toward such a perspective.

The practical details of this step have been worked out in their initial stages by Dr. Eugene T. Gendlin.

Through therapeutic research, he and his colleagues have indirectly opened an extraordinary doorway into the realm of spiritual awareness. His pioneering effort called *Focusing*[2] is a simple way of attending to meaning that is felt in the body.

We believe that the regular use of Focusing can support significant movement toward a humane valuing process. This is valuing that is not drawn from the mind's distinction between right and wrong but from a deeper sense for direction, purpose, and context within the cosmos. There is support within our bodies for unitary consciousness. Focusing, we believe, can contribute to a spirituality that nourishes cosmic congruence irrespective of a person's religious affiliation.

Without some practical "look-out point in the universe," world religions and all people who espouse unitive teachings face an indescribably bleak alternative. Unless we can find a way to live these noble teachings, unless we take concrete steps *to put our bodies where our good intentions are,* unless we discover some path through the barrier of impotence that so impedes progress in religion today, we risk falling victim to the growing technology of planetary destruction. Focusing touches the feelings of fear, frustration, and lack of presence that nourish the suspicions, mistrust, and hatreds that inevitably lead toward war.

The way ahead, of course, lies within ourselves. But discovering the lookout point means learning *to be* in each day, in each passing moment according to the truth and actuality of its *connectedness.* To find this spiritual dimension within ourselves we must first know the truth of how we really *feel* about things, people, and events. We must touch those deeper meanings that our bodies express.

There is a *felt* truth, a *felt* meaning, a *felt* direction within each of us, an embodied sense that can free us and guide us into the future. In-touch living *connects!* It allows values and behavior to change. This is what we mean by bio-spirituality.

Both of us find that Focusing helps us reach this inner knowing. It enables us to sort out our experiences when things are not *right* at a deeper level than that which our intellects can perceive. When reason can only guess at the cause—and not always accurately—our body's awareness of meaning can offer us a direction for change from inside. *Thinking* so often gets in the way of those felt shifts wherein the real cause of alienation, destructive behavior, pain, and confusion can begin to dissipate.

The religions and spiritual movements of the world must step beyond doctrines into this realm of bodily experience, risky though it may seem. What lies ahead will transform old identities and unseat many sacred idols. It will overturn what had formerly been touched only by risking the wrath of the gods.

But if this step can be taken, we believe it will mark the beginning of a new age in human believing. A believing born of change! Discovering a lookout point in the universe may quite literally "renew the face of the earth." The world's religions might even become less competitive, less aggressive, less a source of division between individuals and a block to global wholeness.

The decision making of nations is always a human process. When people begin to touch the deeper unity that can be sensed in their bodies, they will be less likely to choose the path of nuclear destruction. Beyond the darkness of egoism lies an innate sociability and goodness which, through Focusing, can break through to the light of day. To the extent that more and more people break *through* the blockages that hinder the unfolding of their own unique life-meaning, to that extent they will discover a personal freedom and *choice* when they confront the issue of nuclear proliferation. People out of touch with themselves have no real alternative than to constantly prepare for war. Anyone in conflict with himself or herself must inevitably view the world in exactly the same manner. Inner tensions, conflicts and struggles are projected outward into the life of our planet. Multiplied over and over, the momentum of massive inner frustration becomes, finally, in our time the horror of possible nuclear holocaust.

Focusing can address this critical issue of thwarted human meaning. It unveils an inner spiritual resource that is compatible with the unitive teachings and goals of most world religions and philosophies.

Given such a perspective, the two of us, year by year, continue to evaluate our own religious practices, beliefs, and tradition. Much has not measured up. Much has seemed off-the-track and actually harmful to this journey. But we have also discovered something that certainly exists in other traditions as well. Woven into the patrimony of our past lie intriguing clues and revelations about what it means to be human. An exciting, profound invitation to journey farther into our humanity emerges as we continue to explore the roots of our own religious heritage.

In this book we will describe some of these invitations. They tell us far more about ourselves than they tell us about God. There is wisdom here, wisdom we all need as citizens of this planet and cosmos—no matter what our religious or nonreligious orientation.

The deeper *felt meaning* behind special words within our Christian revelation can help everyone, believer and nonbeliever alike, to uncover an inner resource, a broadened *psychological* sense for what it means to be human. There is a bigger picture within bodily knowing. Human awareness is only the opening movement within the vast symphonic arrangement that draws consciousness forward. There is a world beyond ego that transcends all of our foot-dragging resistance. There is *withinness* that uncovers a startling new identity. The roots of individual awareness are far broader than any limited canvas upon which they happen to be painted! We each say "I" out of a vast reservoir that as yet we only dimly perceive. Within the unfolding inwardness of humankind one senses a growing readiness for a momentous new birth.

Teilhard de Chardin suggested that we need some "lookout point in the universe" if we are to light our halting steps into the next phase of human evolution. Just such a Rosetta Stone now lies at hand. It is a unique quality of knowing that lies within our very bodies. It is a *felt sense* of a Larger Consciousness *that is already in place!*

There lies the key. We can never reason or think our way across the next evolutionary horizon. Rather, we must follow some deeper, organic rhythm. An inner resonance. The *felt sense* of Greater Awakening.

The two of us reached a turning point in our own journey when we gradually realized that certain revelations and theological teachings in the Judeo-Christian tradition appear to be aimed not at the mind's purely rational understanding of truth but at some deeper *organismic knowing* based on the *integration* of body and mind.

Theology speaks *about* God. But in order to appreciate the rich *humanistic* impact of such truths, one must draw on more experience than one can think in the mind. *Body knowing, then, when integrated with mind knowing becomes a Rosetta Stone with which to unlock the hidden evolutionary significance of latent bio-spiritual clues hidden within the Judeo-Christian tradition and, no doubt, within other religious traditions as well.*

Perhaps now, more than at any other time in human history, the scientific and religious communities have reached a stage in their separate development where they can finally *cooperate* in the challenging exploration of bodily knowing. Our own humanity has at last become a rich ground for dialogue. A latent perspective waits to be born. But this next forward step requires the convergence of science and religion. In the words of Teilhard de Chardin:

Religion and science are the two conjugated faces or phases of one and the same act of complete knowledge—the only one which can embrace the past and future of evolution so as to contemplate, measure and fulfill them.[3]

Among North American psychologists, Abraham Maslow was intrigued by the potential for spiritual development that lies within a more open and cooperative relationship between religion and science. The flame of his vision, though, was fanned by what he regarded as the sheer *organicity* of spiritual valuing within the person.

My thesis is, in general, that new developments in psychology are forcing a profound change in our philosophy of science, a change so extensive that we may be able to accept the basic religious questions as a proper part of the jurisdiction of science, once science is broadened and redefined.

A whole school of psychologists now believe that "spiritual values" are in the organism, so much a part of the well-functioning organism as to be *sine qua non "defining-characteristics"* of it.

This thesis that religious experiences are natural experiences could be seen by churchmen with dismay, as simply and only a further instance of science carving another chunk out of the side of organized religion—which, of course, it is. But it is also possible for a more perceptively religious man to greet this development with enthusiasm, when he realizes that what the mystics have said to be essential to the *individual's* religion is now receiving empirical support and no longer needs rest only on tradition, blind faith, temporal power, exhortation, etc. If this development is a secularizing of all religion, it is also a religionizing of all that is secular.[4]

The growth of a bio-spiritual perspective must draw on the wisdom of ancient religious traditions as well as on the contemporary appreciation of what it means to be human. In the following pages we will attempt a rough mapping out of several areas where a suitably broadened human science may be enriched by contributions from the Judeo-Christian tradition.

Bodily knowing, for us, is a bridge that links the two realms of science and religion. It can be a common ground where each of these two different approaches can shed some of their limitations and discover together that "act of complete knowledge" that may ultimately fulfill them both.

What, then, are some of the clues hidden within a developing human science as well as within the Judeo-Christian tradition, clues wherein any seeking person can find an openness in bodily knowing? Where are the points of resonance, the organismic windows through which the early dawn of a new creation may rouse the sleeping night of ego? How can such clues encourage a *bio-spiritual positioning* for the next leap forward in human evolution?

Imagine the numbing frustration that must have aggravated their research as early scholars pored over unintelligible hieroglyphics in the Egyptian language. The pictographic script before them provided little support for unravelling the richer message that it contained. Those long-suffering men and women who labored to decipher that baffling code remained quite literally *outside* the meaning they so eagerly sought.

But with the Rosetta Stone in hand, a fog started to lift. Small bits and pieces of meaning began to emerge from the maddening riddle. First, probably, came proper names and places; these were soon followed by individual nouns and verbs, until, finally, entire sentences and paragraphs yielded their long-sought treasures. At last, the world *within* had opened up.

In a similar fashion, one finds special words within the Judeo-Christian tradition, words meant to convey far more than meaning to the mind. Hidden within is a language whose full impact may only be realized to the extent that bodily knowing becomes part of our overall experience. It is a language designed to highlight shades of felt meaning that can arise from any person's inward depth of bodily knowing. But to discover such riches one must first embark upon a deliberate incarnation—*that perilous leap into the body which Christian spirituality is supposed to be all about!*

Yet all of us, Christian and non-Christian alike, hold back from this step beyond reason and control. There is an inner shrinking from the risks involved. It's much like our resistance to falling in a dream. Focusing draws us into a wilderness area within ourselves. It can at first appear to be a place of dark foreboding. One recalls those terrible warnings that were sometimes found on ancient mariners' maps. Beyond the outer fringes of exploration were inscribed those fearsome words: "Traveller beware—Here there be Dragons!"

At this point we experience the last stand of the ego. There is an unwillingness to let go of the identity and security that we have fashioned so laboriously through the careful exercise of reason and control. But unless the seed falls into the ground and dies, there can be no new life. The religious traditions of the world speak to this tension between the satisfactions of limited identity and some farther evolutionary horizon toward which our humanness seems to be called.

For many years now, the two of us have sought to identify the elements that are essential for a bio-spirituality. It is important to realize that we have not been seeking gimmicks or techniques of transformation. Rather we want to understand how the opening of broader bio-spiritual horizons can spontaneously occur as a gratifying component within human development itself. We want to shed light upon a gifted inner ecology. Our personal challenge has been to identify a kind of experiencing that might serve as a link, a point of connection, or the most effective avenue of entry into what Abraham Maslow once described as "the farther reaches of human nature."

1

A leap into bodily knowing

Has it ever struck you that there really are no satisfactory *explanations* for suffering and death? Logic and reason crumble before blind catastrophes and those other senseless tragedies that litter our evolutionary journey. Stripped of all power by such occurrences, the rational mind becomes mute and helpless, like an inarticulate spectator at a funeral.

Perhaps this is because suffering, tragedy, and death really have no satisfactory intellectual explanations. Beyond all logic and reason, their true depth is rarely touched except through the body's appreciation of some deeper meaning and connectedness.

The key goal in spirituality and human evolution is to develop a consciousness potential within the *entire* human organism. Cut off from the knowing that is proper to our bodies, we lose that integral awareness through which we can resonate as living cells within a Larger Cosmic Organism.

Bio-spirituality is growing in an experience of this greater connectedness. It is a term we use to identify the *body* element in spirituality, a knowing that is beyond what reason and the brain can think. The *bio-* in bio-spirituality defines an area within our experience that we feel is an essential ingredient for any spiritual journey.

Bio- recognizes that the knowing proper to our bodies is an immediate inner doorway to the gifted story of some greater At-Homeness that lies within an even Larger Body of Awareness.

Perhaps we need adversity to thrust us beyond the narrow perceptions that blind us to these broader currents. Tragedies, as well as the other mysteries of life, are never *solved* by our intellects but *resolved* in our bodies through an organic inner wisdom. Becoming lost when there are no more rational answers forces us, finally, to launch deeper into ourselves.

But what is bodily knowing? Toward what experience in ourselves must we look in order to find that special vista on some Larger Awareness? We will begin our search in this chapter by considering two questions: "How do we lose touch with bodily knowing in the first place?" and "How can we recover it without sacrificing or abandoning the obvious benefits of intellect and reason?"

As a start toward answering the first question, you might recall some examples from long ago of how you learned to block your body's knowing. As children we were all hurt by people and by circumstances. We felt scared, angry, confused, frightened, and insecure. These feelings were in our bodies, and we felt them physically. Our bodies hurt and sometimes we cried. As adults, we may not even remember some of these early, painful experiences. *But our bodies remember.* The hurt is still there, lodged deep within us.

Have you ever met people who twenty, thirty, or even fifty years after they have been wronged still *feel* exactly the same way about the aggravating person or situation? By retelling their stories they relive the entire episode again. All the old feelings are torn open once more. Their hurt has never changed or moved in any way. The old battle wounds remain unhealed.

We all know people like that. They recount their bad experiences with as much energy as if they had just happened yesterday. Without realizing it, they might have told us the same story many times before. But they launch into it once again, so intense are the feelings still generated by the retelling. They try to flush some aggravating negativity out of their systems by repeatedly recounting how they had been wronged. But it doesn't work.

What happened to many of these people and to many of us as children is that no one ever taught us *how to be in our hurt* so that it could unfold into a better place, a better feeling, and therefore into a better experience of our bodies. Usually we grew to experience negative feelings as bad, something to be avoided because they made our bodies feel bad and hurt. Most of us concluded that if we were to avoid experiencing a hurting body, then we had to avoid experiencing the kinds of feelings that made it hurt. So we adopted various strategies to avoid coming to grips with bodily knowing. Some of us learned to *distance* ourselves from our feelings. We became masters at distracting ourselves from pain; we created our own little worlds in the spaces between our dealings with other people.

But there is no way that some events in our lives won't hurt us. Feelings of anger, jealousy, fright, and guilt will sweep over us. They simply happen.

Yet as soon as they do, we usually push them away. We try to get rid of them or repress them. We seek ways to flush such painful emotions out of our systems. Anything to bring peace and calm so our bodies will feel better.

Rarely, though, have we been taught *how to be in the hurt,* allowing it to say something about life and ourselves, letting it tell its own unique story.

Most of us *never allowed hurts to unfold.* We closed off an entire dimension of ourselves. Rather than being supported in working through our pain, the process was usually aborted. We might easily have developed a habit of denying or not listening to our feelings, and the distress in our bodies could easily have grown from this. At times, we might even have developed an attitude of not wanting to feel much of anything for fear of feeling something bad. We may have gradually closed off our ability or our need to listen to our bodies. Generally, this was done not only from fear of experiencing something bad, but also from fear of re-experiencing all the old hurts that were never allowed to unfold in the first place.

Deep down, though, our bodies know that this unprocessed experiencing is still there. Each of us instinctively realizes this, and we are usually reluctant to resurrect it. As a result, the entire area of feeling anything can become extremely risky for some people.

It is no wonder, then, that much of every day's experiencing is lived almost exclusively in our heads. Such rejection of bodily knowing eventually takes its toll, however. We suffer and break down physically and emotionally. As someone once said, mental illness is brought on not because we have "gone out of our minds" but because we are "too much in them"! We become cut off from a more integral way of knowing reality and knowing ourselves. We are cut off from the human values and perceptions rooted in our bodies that enable us to live on this planet without destroying everything around us. The origins of violence and potential planetary destruction lie deep within such alienation from ourselves.

Mother Teresa, the Nobel Peace Prize recipient, recently said something that caught our attention. She observed that society knows, in general, what to do for the hungry, the naked, and the sick. But she sensed a far more radical poverty, especially in the West. It is subtle and more difficult to transform. Food, clothing, and all the bandages in the world can never touch the widespread frustration, anxiety, loneliness, anger, and depression that permeate our culture. This requires a different kind of healing.

What makes Focusing unusual is that it creates an inner climate around our painful and frightening issues that is different from the climate we generally fall into with problems and difficulties. Normally, we feel bad about things we don't like in ourselves. We sometimes feel ashamed, guilty, annoyed, or impatient. We hold at arm's length and try to control what we cannot accept. Focusing invites us to relate in a different way to what we perceive as unlovable in ourselves.

"Can I find some way to be a little more *friendly* with my feelings that are so hard to deal with?" This is a vital element in the Focusing process. Being friendly usually doesn't solve the problem right away, but it is a special way of being more gentle, more open, less argumentative, and more kind with a hurting place in ourselves. This allows us, sometimes for the very first time, to really feel our problem as we carry it in a bodily way. Most of us only feel our uncomfortableness with a problem or our need to control it. Rarely, however, do we experience what it is like deliberately and consciously to be *in* the body's sense of negative issues without immediately being pressured either to control or eliminate whatever hurting, scary, or other feelings are there. This openness to bodily knowing within the Focusing process sets the stage for real and sometimes dramatic change as hurting places are allowed to unfold.

This brings us to our second question: "How can we recover a more integral connection with bodily knowing?"

Several years ago during a workshop the two of us conducted with Dr. Eugene Gendlin, one of our participants raised a question about negative hurts and feelings. Her point was that she found it relatively easy to be present to positive feelings of joy, excitement, love, tenderness, curiosity, and so on. But anger, depression, guilt, loneliness, frustration, and a desire for revenge—these she found more difficult.

Dr. Gendlin's response challenged her to adopt a new perspective. He replied: "You must learn to be with your negative feeling *as you would be with a hurting child*."

The image was graphic. To sit down with hostility, fear, or grief, and deliberately put your arm around some thing in yourself which for years you might have held at arm's length was quite a challenge. Almost like going to bed with the devil!

This called to mind tales of the Senoi, an isolated jungle folk who live on the Malay Peninsula. Parents in this tribe have a marvelous way of counseling their children when the little ones have nightmares. Rather than just comforting them after such a frightening experience, the parents open another possibility by suggesting: "Oh, that's an opportunity. It's really the best kind of dream you can have!"

The child, obviously, doesn't think it was so nice. Nightmares of falling, for example, are ordinarily very scary. But the mother and father persist: "When you fall in a dream, you're really falling into a *deeper place in yourself*. It is the place from which a Great Spirit speaks. Someday you will recall these words right inside your dream. Then, letting yourself go into this fearful adventure, you will come face to face with a wonderful surprise!"

The message of these examples, both in our workshop and in the Senoi approach to dreams is essentially the same. Allow yourself to be fully in the bodily knowing of your unacceptable, fearful experience, and it will unfold a surprising story— usually quite different from what reason might lead you to expect.

During one of our recent workshops we mentioned the Senoi and their approach to dreams. After the session a woman came forward, excited at what she had heard and wanting to share a similar experience. As a child she had always been told that if she failed to awaken before reaching the bottom of her dream fall, she would die! Later, as an adult, she endured a prolonged period during which she experienced many nightmares of falling. She had dreams from which she would awaken terrified with her heart pounding.

One night, however, as the familiar nightmare returned and she found herself beginning to fall, she made the deliberate decision *inside her dream* to let go and allow herself to drop. She recalled being over some European village. Clearly visible below her were the tiled roofs of homes and buildings nestled together in a narrow valley. The ground rushed up toward her at a dizzying pace. All the while she knew she could stop this terrible experience by just waking up. The temptation was great to do so. "The roofs got closer and closer," she said. "The ground came up faster and faster." "And finally," she exclaimed, "I hit!" Then, turning her eyes wide with amazement, she asked: "Can you guess what happened?"

"I bounced! A glorious, easy, airy, delight-filled bounce. But even more important," she confided, "up to the present day I have *never again* experienced that terrible nightmare!"

She had *become* her falling. By *owning* this dimension of her being, *allowing* the bodily felt sense of it to unfold, she had stumbled upon a surprising doorway. It was an entry point of transformation in the way her body carried a hurting past experience.

For a moment now, put yourself in the place of a Senoi child who has just emerged from a nightmare. The thought of going back and *letting go* into a dream fall rather than fighting to gain control of or stopping your descent through waking up would be a terrifying prospect, wouldn't it?

Or, would it? Recall your worst nightmare. Are you perhaps just a little intrigued at what might have happened had you been able to just *let go* in such a situation and not try to control or escape?

The transition to such risk-taking, however, is rarely easy. The New Testament speaks of *metanoia*—conversion. A step beyond control. It is often frightening, but it's challenging as well. Conversion leads gradually toward possessing more and more of your self! It involves letting go of controls that hold you to a narrow and often confining experience. There is the challenge of a hidden surprise. A gift. A grace waiting in the uncertainty of that overpowering darkness from which we generally shield ourselves.

We recall another dream we once shared between the two of us. In this particular nightmare, Peter was suddenly confronted by a terrifying, bearded man. A powerful Old Testament-like figure robed in a cloak and filled with wrath who glared and shouted like a threatening ayatollah.

Pete's initial reaction was one of traumatic fear and a desperate effort to flee. But then he stopped short, and recalled within his own dream the story about the Senoi.

At that point he too deliberately turned, and with a good deal of inner trembling he slowly advanced toward what appeared to be certain harm. The closer he approached, the angrier the bearded figure became. The intensity of his rage was almost more than Pete could bear. But his determination held. Saying nothing, he walked forward until he was face to face with the figure. Then came the surprise.

Without any warning this terrifying apparition suddenly broke down and began to weep; it shriveled up at the same time into a very little and feeble old man. It was a stunning experience, one which Peter will never forget.

The important point here is not "What does the dream mean?" Our reason for recalling these vivid episodes is to illustrate a letting go of the reins that must be practiced regularly *while a person is fully awake and alert*. It is a counterculture commitment to the sometimes frightening act of consciously letting ourselves fall into our entire organism's awareness of each moment.

Dreams like these made us wonder. Could there be a deliberate, wide-awake way to *position* ourselves so that we could be drawn inside whatever was real, even though it was fearful or difficult?

Is it not strange that most of us resist this *letting go* into what our bodies know about something? We are reluctant to try anything beyond the mind's logical, reasoned approach to problem solving. We avoid this alternate path, finding any excuse to distract ourselves from growing quiet and attending to what our whole being, especially our bodies, can tell us about how things are right now.

Few of us believe that such bodily knowing can express an awesome invitation to the benevolent wisdom and grace of the cosmos. It is frightening to let go of the reins. Most people suffer such vulnerability only as a desperate last resort. We doubt the possibility of survival. Resurrection in such circumstances is quite literally *beyond* reason.

Yet there is wisdom in our bodies! A sure-footed sense for deeper meaning, purpose, and direction.

But this wisdom lies behind an obscuring veil within ourselves. Perhaps it is like a screen falling at the farther edge of reason. Possibly our mind itself is the veil. No matter what, the letting go required to pass beyond this barrier contradicts all of our cultural conditioning and educational programming.

This is because human transformation depends upon far more than information. The critical factor for change is not *understanding* but an experience of give, shift, or *movement* in the bodily awareness of a problem or life situation. This is not seeing new things; it's a new way of seeing! It is an experience of inner *release*. This is what counts and what makes real change in awareness possible.

The difficulty, of course, is that this kind of release always flies with wings of unpredictability. It seldom arrives on schedule. It has an air of haphazardness and it eludes programmed control; it comes more like a *gift*, a grace.

We don't *make* the human story unfold. Our bodily-felt carrying of this next step cannot be hurried along through pre-planned control and engineering. It must be *allowed* to come into existence.

Loosening the reins of this control and letting ourselves experience such graced wisdom are two essential ingredients of bio-spirituality. They open a way of being in ordinary awareness, scary or joyful, which allows the shadowy places as well as the happy ones to tell their stories. Here, finally, we can find a doorway into a realm of greater freedom and a sense for a larger At-Homeness that may help us avoid the perilous shoals of potential nuclear holocaust.

Let us turn, then, to the practical details of what we will now call *the art of allowing*.

2

Learning to focus

Practical steps toward the art of allowing

What does it feel like inside to let go of the reins? What part of you gets involved? Toward what kind of experiencing is it best to direct your attention? What can you do? What can you *not* do to support an unfolding of your own bio-spiritual perspective? Let's turn now to some practical steps in the art of allowing.

In this chapter we will describe our approach to Focusing. After that we will begin to sketch a broader vision, situating the art of allowing within a framework of evolutionary spirituality. We will probe that inviting frontier in ourselves that Teilhard de Chardin sought to describe. Ultimately we want to peer into the depth of a bio-spirituality that draws both us and our world into a ripening Mystery of cosmic congruence.

But first we must learn a method or an approach to bodily knowing. Taking one step at a time then, let's reconsider those hurts we described in chapter 1, hurts which our bodies can never forget.

So many people simply go around in circles with their negative feelings. Having never learned to get beneath an emotion into the wider bodily felt sense of a problem, they remain locked in self-defeating patterns. Instead of ongoing change that would refresh their inner landscapes, the same stale emotional responses recur with frustrating regularity. These people live with more or less rigid, pre-programmed *reactions* to specific situations and people. Given a particular stimulus, they always feel the *same kind* of anger, the same resentful hurt, or the same recurring sense of inferiority. A well-worn record plays over and over again. There is no bodily felt release within which to experience change. There is no inner *resolution* of their tiresome, debilitating response.

From a therapeutic point of view, Eugene Gendlin's unique contribution has been to show that surface emotions, whether positive or negative, are directly tied to a more rudimentary *felt sense* of how a particular issue is carried in the body. Successful therapy has something to do with a refreshing release in this area of experiencing.

Gendlin found meaning beyond the mind. There is *felt* meaning as well, a meaning that is known and carried in the body. This meaning is different from that which we think. Not that such *bodily* meaning is unintelligible, it just *behaves* differently from the meanings that we can conceptualize.

This remains a rather vague area for most of us. We can usually identify our more obvious feelings and emotions. But the deeper felt meanings tied in with such emotions are less readily available to our ordinary awareness. At least we don't *attend* to them with the same facility and discipline with which we solve practical everyday problems.

Words like *fear, anger, resentment,* and *joy* say something in general about certain feelings that we all have. These words are useful tools for communication. But the universal term *anger* never completely describes the uniquely personal flavor of *my* anger. *Anger* is a generic word. It refers to anger in general, just as *flower* names the blossom of any plant without specifying that which differentiates it as totally unique—*this* red rosebud.

My anger is always more than just anger in general. It has a specific texture that includes an initially nameless, somewhat tangled mass of inner, bodily felt meaning that colors *this* anger as uniquely my own. The more readily observable outburst of emotion is only the tip of an iceberg.

Eugene Gendlin has referred to the broader substratum beneath this visible tip as a *felt sense*. This term embraces a wider, initially nebulous meaning that is felt rather than conceptualized in our awareness. It is called *felt* because it is felt in the body. It is called *sense,* not like the five senses, but more like *the sense of something* or *he makes good sense. Sense,* here, has a meaning that is felt—as yet unclear and vague. It is a meaning that is felt in the body rather than known in the mind.

As Gendlin points out, to feel "unaccountably uncomfortable" means you are aware of more in your body than you can think in your mind. That is a felt sense, and it is always more than what you may have immediate words or rational explanations for. In fact, it is often a clear sign of a *felt sense* when you definitely experience something without yet having the right word or symbol for it.

The felt sense, then, is rarely reason-logical. It is rather body-logical. Its meaning will not fit easily into the categories of cause and effect. The felt sense exhibits surprising twists and turns; it almost seems to have a different function than the meanings we think with our minds. This is why we said earlier that it behaves differently.

As an example, we recall one workshop in which a woman began to focus, and immediately she felt overwhelmed by sadness and tears without in any way knowing why or what this was all about. Her body felt sadness, yet her mind could in no way understand or explain why she had such a feeling. She needed time to be with this felt sense until it could unfold a deeper story. The story, it turned out, was quite different from what she consciously thought about certain issues in her life. Her body realized something that she had never allowed herself to become aware of in her head.

The felt sense, then, does not seem to be directed toward solutions in our intellects but toward a *resolution* in the way our bodies carry certain issues and concerns in our lives. Its function has something to do with a special movement or release within the realm of organismic rather than exclusively mental knowing.

But what is this movement, and how does it take place? What triggers this transformation?

In pursuing this elusive resolution, Dr. Gendlin decided not to work directly with surface emotions. Rather, using the procedure called Focusing, he found that a person could be taught to move his or her awareness *through* an emotion deeper into the bodily felt awareness of a problem. The more easily identifiable surface emotion is *not* the principal lever that facilitates a change. It represents, rather, a vital *doorway* into that realm of experiencing where change can occur—much like the nightmare for the Senoi child revealed an unexpected depth of spirit.

What, then, are the basic instructions for Focusing? Since it is an art that can only be fully appreciated in the actual doing of it, our goal in the following pages is not to offer a practical manual on how to focus. This has already been done by Dr. Gendlin in his book called *Focusing*.[1]

We find that the technique aspect of Focusing is best learned from someone who is experienced in the method and who regularly practices it in his or her life. Books or manuals about Focusing can be useful tools in this learning process. They are especially helpful, and in some instances may even substitute for a good teacher, when the learner knows how to make that vital leap between information on the printed page and what is actually occurring within his or her own experience. When a person instinctively *knows* what an author is writing about, not as information but through a sense of *having been there themselves*—then learning can go forward. If this should happen in your reading of what follows, so much the better. But we set a more modest goal for ourselves.

We simply want to provide you with some appreciation for how your inner story might unfold. We wish to heighten your awareness of how your body speaks its own unique language, and how destructive patterns of feeling can be resolved. These pages are primarily an invitation to look further into yourself.

If anything, our aim is motivational. By carefully attending to certain experiences you could be led toward that gifted inner stream where the sense for being bodily alive in some Larger Process can unfold. This broader bio-spiritual enterprise is our principal concern. Let's consider, then, the process of Focusing as one promising approach to this inviting inner world.

There are certain steps that anyone can follow when first learning to focus. These steps are taught in different ways by different teachers. What we now wish to share is the way *we* teach Focusing. It is not the only way. We just find that it has worked well for the two of us. Once a person achieves a certain familiarity with the process, some of the initial steps may occasionally be dropped. We encourage beginners to go through the entire series, however, because it provides a useful framework within which to learn one's own unique pattern and language of unfolding.

Our approach in this chapter will be to describe each step of Focusing and then to comment on it in some detail. We will share experiences and examples that we find help us and our workshop participants learn to Focus. Once we have completed this more lengthy description, we will summarize at the end of the book, the basic steps so that anyone may readily use them either when Focusing alone or when helping someone else.

We should note here that Focusing can be greatly facilitated by the caring presence of another person. This must, however, be a presence that never seeks to intrude or to force any predetermined agenda on the one Focusing. A good facilitator simply "walks along" with the focuser, providing support and minimal assistance for the direction and the surprise that can emerge from within the person who is actually doing the Focusing.

Let's turn, then, to the steps involved in this process. We call the first step *Finding a Space by Taking an Inventory*.

A person usually begins Focusing by taking a moment to step back from the ongoing rush of thinking and emotion that fills so much of every day. This is like a quick breather that serves as a prelude to what follows next. This initial moment is perhaps best understood by realizing what it is *not*. It is not relaxing! It is not seeking some deep place for meditation and quiet or a brief escape.

If something is bothering you, if you have a nagging inner felt sense clamoring for attention, you don't want to lose it or dull it by first getting nice and comfortable. No. The initial stepping back is meant to *sharpen* any bodily awareness that may be there ready to be focused upon.

What you seek in this opening moment of Focusing is to back off from the usually jumbled stream of feelings and thoughts inside of you so that you are not overwhelmed by confusion. You don't back away from what needs to be focused upon; you back away from *the mixing up* of that with a whole lot of other things that may currently be occupying your attention.

What you want to do in this opening moment is allow your attention to drop downward into the feeling part of yourself. Sometimes it helps just to close your eyes and ask yourself something like this: "How am I right now?" Let the answer to that question rise from deep within you, not as a thinking but as a feeling. Give yourself a moment to break away from your ordinary problem-solving, rational, worrying self, and just attend to your body's knowing right now.

While growing quiet inside, let your attention settle toward the center of your body—the solar plexus region. We encourage people to include awareness of this area in their bodies right at the beginning of Focusing because it often helps them notice more easily how their bodies are carrying life issues. After a few moments of turning your awareness inward in this way, ask yourself the following question: "Is there anything keeping me from feeling really good right now?"

Sit with that question for a while and see what comes.

The question may cause an image to pop into your head or a memory to return. Perhaps a hunch may come forward. Something that has been bothering you may finally surface, or a queasy feeling might arise in your stomach. Notice, in particular, your inner response to the question. How does your body carry whatever keeps you from feeling really good right now? For example, is there a tightness in your chest? Perhaps, an aching loneliness? Maybe you notice a vague feeling of being chained down, suffocating, or always being rushed by the pace of your life. Allow yourself a few moments to notice the felt sense side of whatever comes in response to that question.

Once you have identified something, don't try to do anything with it. Don't spend time feeling bad about it, trying to solve it, or figuring it out. Just notice whatever comes. Then, if you can, gently put it aside for the time being.

Give yourself a moment in which to sense what it feels like to set this down beside you and not be carrying it within you. Then, if you can do this, ask yourself another question: "If this were all resolved, would there be anything else between me and feeling really fine right now?"

It may be that the first feeling that comes is so painful or up front that you can't set it aside and continue. If that happens, then go on to what we will call Step Three in the Focusing process.

Usually, however, if what comes up is not all that preoccupying, it can be set aside temporarily in order to see whether something else lies between you and feeling really good at that moment.

Some interesting things can happen when you ask the further question: "If this were all resolved, would there be anything else between me and feeling fine right now?" Occasionally, an unexpected bodily carrying of an additional issue will emerge when you ask this question. Generally, when you pose the first question about what's keeping you from feeling really good right now, your body's sense for some *current* concern will surface. Not always, of course, but more often than not. Then when this is momentarily set aside, there is room for more subtle shades of body awareness to emerge; awareness, we might add, which is not always dark or difficult or bad. An unrealized excitement can often surface. You may occasionally be surprised by more profound life issues that have gotten lost in the flurry of daily activities.

What you are doing in this unusual bodily felt inventory is gradually working your way toward an open space in yourself that lies on the other side of all the felt issues that remain unresolved at this time. Many people who eventually reach that space often find that it opens into an important spiritual experience for them. They discover a kind of inner widening of self. Having set down, for a moment, their burden of difficult things, they detect a glimmer of some spiritual "more" that momentarily refreshes their inner being.

But this is *not* the immediate goal of the first step in Focusing. If it should happen, that's fine. But what we are about is something quite different. At this early point in the Focusing process, we simply want to give our bodies a chance to surface the largely unnoticed *carrying* of life that lies within us at every waking moment.

So some people may find it helpful to repeat several times: "If this were all resolved, then could I feel really fine right now, or would there still be something between me and feeling OK?" As often as some further issue arises, notice it, then gently set it aside to see if anything else wants to come forward. In this way you will be taking an inventory in which your goal is nothing more than to *identify* what is there without attempting to *do* anything with it.

Sometimes when people ask the first question: "Is anything keeping me from feeling really good right now?" the answer may be "No!" That's a special moment for anyone if it should happen. No negative or unresolved body feeling surfaces to claim our attention. Whenever this happens, you can then ask: "Are there any other things in my life right now, not necessarily problems, that it would be good to get in touch with?" This is also a question you may ask after you've noticed and set aside whatever keeps you from feeling really good right now.

This second part of your inventory provides an opportunity to review other important issues in your life in addition to the more vague or troublesome feelings that may have surfaced initially. It is not always necessary to ask this further question, unless, of course, you find that nothing particularly bothersome came into your awareness when you first checked to see if anything stood between you and feeling really good right now.

What this further question does, if you use it, is to allow a wider range of issues, feelings, and concerns—both positive and negative—to come forward and identify themselves. Once again, the goal is not to begin fretting over worrisome items in your line-up. This is simply an opportunity to take stock of what is there. You're conducting an *inventory*—nothing more, nothing less.

One suggestion we always make to participants in our workshops, though, is to be on the lookout for unexpected elements that may pop into their inventories by surprise. Most of the time we think we know what our primary issues, problems, and concerns are. But the questions we ask in setting the stage for Focusing involve far more than a rational exercise done with our heads. We must remain open for our body's knowing to come in and suggest things. After a little practice, you'll gradually recognize subtle ways in which this occurs.

Usually what happens is that some uninvited element flies by on the periphery of your consciousness. It may be an image, the memory of some painful or embarrassing situation, or per-haps an unexpected anticipation of something that will happen tomorrow. You must be alert to catch these little surprises as they flit by on the edge of your awareness.

Do you know what peripheral vision is like? Catching some movement out of the corner of your eye. The appearance of bodily knowing is often like that. But when you have spent years attending primarily to what can be thought in your mind, it's easy to miss these marginal clues. They slip by without being noticed.

Soon, however, as you begin to recognize them, and especially as you discover how they can really be treasures leading toward a deeper resolution in bodily knowing, you will value them and attend more carefully to their appearance.

Moreover, you'll occasionally find random details popping into your awareness that seem to have little connection with anything either at a thinking or a body-feeling level. First check to see if they have a *feeling of importance*. If not, just let them slip by. Should they be really significant and you lose them, they'll eventually come back.

The real effort in this first step must be to remain open to whatever seems to be *most up front* for you right now in your life. This can include items that are big or small, long-term or relatively recent, good or bad. Remember that the inventory is not just picking out problems and hurts. It's allowing *anything* that happens to have a kind of here-and-now organismic energy to come forward and be recognized. This can include major life decisions and situations, small pinpricks and bright spots that have occurred in the last day, or little surprises that come uninvited as though from nowhere.

The point of this first step in Focusing is not to make an exhaustive catalogue of every possible memory, hurt, or expectation that might figure in to your current sense of self. Try to regard this initial exercise like the cream that used to rise to the top of the old milk bottles. You're just trying to get the main things, the cream off the top. Should you miss something, don't worry about it. If it's really important, it will come up again some other time.

There is an amazing wisdom within the human organism. It knows more about the "way home to ourselves" than we can ever think in our heads. It knows where all the inner blockages are that stand in the way of growing, and it has enough sense to move the "big ones" forward in their proper time and sequence so that a resolution may occur.

Finding a Space by Taking an Inventory provides your body with a chance to speak. It lets whatever lies between you and some larger picture come to the surface and identify itself. The surprising thing, however, is that the very items that rise into awareness as apparent obstacles and stumbling blocks to spiritual unfolding are, in fact, your most privileged pathways into the Larger Mystery. In this first step of Focusing *you identify doorways!* All those feelings and felt meanings that stand between you and a more open inner space actually contain your body's potential for being drawn further forward into a vast evolutionary unfolding.

None of us can ever *think* our way into bio-spiritual awareness. Rather, we are drawn forward along a path of more integral bodily knowing.

Finally, it helps to look at this first step in Focusing with a generous amount of flexibility. If during the course of your inventory you should come upon something that stands out with a vibrancy and energy that clamors for immediate attention, then maybe that's what you should be with for now. Don't feel compelled to *finish* your inventory before coming back to this matter.

One additional point, too, about that more open inner space, the "feeling really good right now" that lies on the other side of all the bodily-felt obstacles in between. Remember that this space is a developmental experience. It will be different for different people. It will even be different for the same person at different times.

Sometimes the inner space and good feeling will be nothing more than tension reduction. For a person in physical pain, simply to have the agony stop or diminish somewhat is enough. It is a place of rest, a gratifying break in what may be a very trying ordeal. At other times, however, the space may turn into an awe-inspiring place of wonder, a spiritual vista point.

What is important about such a space is that it can provide a bodily-felt experience that reveals that there is more to who you are than the current pain or malaise to which your attention may be narrowed. This is extremely important, especially for someone who usually lives with a constricted sense of self. Such a person desperately needs to find a place of fresh air deep inside.

Even though time may elapse before you actually become congruent with such an experience, it is important to touch that space *at least as a promise of what can be.* Finding this space of feeling good within yourself can serve as a beacon of hope. It can be a light beyond the many obstacles that still stand in the path of finding a way through to some positive core experience. We are reminded of those magnificent lines that close the Genesis creation narrative: "And God saw everything that he had made, *and behold it was very good."(Gen. 1:31, RSV,* emphasis ours) All of us continually seek a bodily-felt sense of that *goodness* that lies at the core of our being. *Finding a Space by Taking an Inventory* can be an important step on this journey into ourselves. Let's now turn to what comes next.

We call the second step of Focusing *Feeling Which One Is Number One.* What you do at this point is to return to the various issues you have identified thus far. Passing before each of them, you now try to gain some feeling for which item stands out as Number One for you *at this precise moment.* Which is the one to spend time with now? What draws you to itself in such a way that you *know* this is the one to focus on?

We emphasize the first word in our description of this step: *Feeling* which is Number One.

Feeling! The discernment that you make at this point is never one of logical judgment or evaluation. It must not be a decision based upon that you think *ought* to be focused upon at this time. No. Take your cue from the inherent power or energy that an item may have for you in this particular moment.

That's why it is often good to ask yourself *feeling questions* like: "Which one is the warmest, the heaviest, the most uncomfortable, the most pressing, the most exciting, and so on." Think of this not as a rational selection process but more like *taking the temperature* of each bodily felt sense until you find one that stands out above all the others.

We had an interesting experience with a participant in one of our workshops that illustrates this point. A man had come to the weekend workshop determined to spend time working on his feelings about his marriage. His agenda was all laid out in advance. But when, during Focusing, he risked allowing his entire organism to reveal what was Number One, something unexpected happened. He realized that what was most up front, apparently, was not at all what he had planned to work on. Rather, it was *his fear of Focusing!* The surprising thing, however, was that when he sat with this issue, allowing it time to symbolize itself, he was also blessed with more resolution in the marriage relationship than he ever would have experienced had he tried to force this earlier agenda upon his bodily knowing.

It helps, then, at this stage in the Focusing process to set all your *oughts* and pre-planned agenda aside. Sometimes the inconsequential, the peripheral, the unexpected becomes your doorway to change.

Recall what we said earlier about felt meaning. It *behaves* differently. It is not mind-logical. There is no way to force a resolution in bodily knowing. You can sometimes override feelings with various coping devices and behavior modification. But lasting change is a gift from within the flow of your own story. Focusing provides an opportunity for such a grace to appear.

If there can be a reverent "sitting down beside" the items of our inventory, then one of them in some uniquely personal fashion will signal a primacy over all the others—at least for now.

Obviously, when you are clearly upset, you *know* right away without any inventory what is Number One. At those times you can simply dispense with these early steps. You can ask yourself: "How am I right now?" With little hesitation the felt sense of that moment will usually come crashing into awareness.

The inventory, however, can be helpful in quieter times. It's also useful when there is such a turmoil of hurting and conflict that sorting things out a bit will help to bring your attention to bear on what lies within. Use whatever approach seems right at any given moment.

Once you have been able to *feel* Number One, you are then ready to move on to the third step. This involves asking a very important question.

Is It OK to Be With This? It is a simple request designed to respect freedom, and it never forces you beyond the control that may be necessary at any given point in your life.

Sometimes what surfaces as Number One may be, for the beginner, too frightening to be with. Maybe it's a long-term, deep-rooted experience, so painful that any proximity is too much to bear. There is usually a great deal of initial fear and healthy scepticism about getting involved with this kind of hurt in ourselves. Perhaps every past attempt to work with pain has resulted in more pain or simply a wallowing in misery. If so, there is usually no positive back-up experience to support risking such an approach again.

Focusing, however, is a radically different way of being with such a difficult blockage in ourselves. But the beginner doesn't yet know this, and he or she should never rashly push past defenses set up to protect against the inner anguish of getting too close. Time and experience will eventually show that this process allows even the deepest kinds of hurt to unfold.

We recall a humorous incident that occurred during a workshop that included among the participants a trained therapist who regularly used Focusing in her own life and professional practice. The timing of this workshop happened to coincide with her own working through a rather painful experience in her life. She was Focusing in a small practice group with others who were just beginning to Focus for the first time. Pete, the facilitator, asked the standard question: "Is it OK to be with all that?" The question was asked as much for the teaching value it had for the rest of the group as for the person to whom it was directed. There was a long pause as the woman struggled back from the depth of her own painful felt sense. Then, cocking her head to the side, she opened one eye and with an exquisitely knowing smile said: "I can be with anything!"

Experience in Focusing always leads beyond the need for permission to go ahead. But in the beginning it is a salutary check point.

What happens, though, if the answer is "No"? What if your sense for Number One is such that you don't want to get within a country mile of it? Then what can you do?

Whenever the Number One item is simply too much to be with for now, you must respect the need for distance. Then try an alternate approach. Open another possibility by asking yourself: "Is it OK to be with the feeling of not wanting to get into all this right now?" Can you Focus on your being afraid of it, too tired to face it, or whatever else happens to express your unique "No" response in such a situation?

Do you see what you're doing by taking this route? You are, first of all, continuing to remain with what is real at the moment, namely, an unwillingness to get involved with this Number One. But remember, all this hanging back has a bodily felt sense associated with it. It's not the big one, but it is an integral part of getting close to this area of major blockage. It is equally part of your process. So, go with it.

By taking this kind of approach you remain within the stream of *real* experiencing without having to tackle your big problem head on. This usually turns out to be a "coming in the back door" on the main issue. Gradually, after a while, you wind your way into it at your own pace.

It might help you to think of your rich inner world of bodily felt meaning as a large embroidered tapestry, like one of those magnificent wall hangings you find in museums. Now imagine that a thread comes loose somewhere on the tapestry. If you pull that thread and follow its unravelling, it will eventually cross other threads that lead into every part of the picture. No matter where you jump in, the thread you follow at that point will sooner or later connect with every important item in the total design.

Focusing is like that! You may begin at some inconsequential little sketch in an obscure corner of the tapestry that is your inner landscape of felt meaning, but eventually you will be drawn through to everything that is inside you! The critical point, however, is *finding the first loose thread!* That's what your inventory and getting the feel of Number One allows you to do. It gives your body a chance to point the way. The threads, remember, are rarely where we *think* they *should* be. They are the loose ends of life, the unfinished in ourselves where doorways yet remain to be opened.

It is important to realize when Focusing that you never play games with yourself. The goal here is more than just coping with bad situations. It is an inner positioning for the gifted possibility of genuine change. You are seeking bodily-felt resolution in the way you carry some problem or issue. This is not just a novel way to feel good for a while. It's not just snatching a bit of rest before lifting again the burdens you wake up with each morning. To Focus means to risk the possibility that each burden may have a chance to tell its own story and in the telling might be changed from within.

There are many doorways leading into this resolution in bodily knowing. It is important to find the one that seems most appropriate for you at any given moment. The guiding principle is always to go with some bodily felt sense that you can touch right now. If it is OK to be with your Number One, even though it might be a little scary, then go with it. If not, then go with *the being scared* about getting into it.

Should you find that your being with a particularly difficult Number One eventually becomes too scary and you want to stop, remember that *you are always the one in charge.* If you want to stop, stop! Or, better, switch over to: "Now this is getting too difficult to get into." See if you can be with that fear of going further, letting it tell its story. Eventually, as you travel along on your inner journey, learning its mysterious and sometimes surprising ways, you, too, may be blessed with that marvelous inner liberation: "I can be with *anything!*"

There is an unexpected resource within the flesh and sinew of bodily knowing, a bio-spiritual aliveness that can draw you well beyond fear into the vitalizing inner sense for *being a new creation!* But we are getting ahead of ourselves.

Once it is OK to be with a felt sense of Number One, then what? We have tried various ways of describing the fourth step in Focusing as we teach it. *Letting Go into It; Just Being In It; Sensing the Whole of It.* Here, the inner stance is not one of trying to figure something out. Thinking is set aside. Reason is appropriate for other tasks, but not for this one. One tries, instead, to remain *inside* the felt sense of Number One.

Have you ever suffered a severe headache or the pain of an arthritic joint? Do you know the inner experience as you try to *distance* yourself from that kind of suffering? The soreness becomes almost an alien force, something that is not you, but attacks you. You try to hold the pain at arm's length, trying to keep it *outside* of your "you." There is an inner shrinking back from the pain, from the soreness that is right within your own body. Perhaps you know something of this attempted dissociation.

But have you ever tried the exact opposite? Moving right into the middle of your pain? Being *inside it* instead of struggling to separate yourself from it. Just letting go into it. Surprises can sometimes occur when you do this.

In the first chapter we wrote about being *friendly* with difficult feelings and issues. Step Four in Focusing is a special way of getting beyond the practice of holding what hurts you at arm's length. If the main thing you're in touch with about a painful feeling or situation is that you don't like it or wish it would go away, then you always remain one step removed from the actual feeling that needs to change. Transformation becomes possible to the extent that you directly touch your felt carrying of an issue and not just your negative feelings about it. This encourages an attitude of open listening to what is really inside you, the hurt, confusion, bitterness, longing, or whatever.

We encourage those who attend our workshops to look for *concrete images* that can help them move beyond always holding what is troublesome at arm's length. Many find Dr. Gendlin's suggestion helpful: imagining that they are holding a painful issue on their lap just as they might hold a hurting child. Others, for whom this is too much, find it helpful to imagine themselves simply resting their hand on whatever hurts inside; this allows a different relationship to emerge. Some find it necessary to locate what bothers them at a distance from themselves, for example, across the room or just outside the door. Such distancing sometimes makes it possible to experience the felt sense of an issue that has been avoided because it is so painful, frightening, or confusing.

Concrete imaging can be helpful because it breaks patterns and creates a different climate around an issue you don't like or have been avoiding inside yourself. This makes it easier, then, to let go into how the issue actually feels in your body. We all tend, in some way, to block out our negative felt sensing. This is usually unintentional, but it can easily become habitual. Using "friendly" imagery helps us be more open inside, allowing hurting places to tell their stories. As this happens, our bodily felt carrying of some painful memory, situation, or feeling can then begin to change.

One humorous illustration of "Letting go into it" comes from our workshop instructions. You know what it's like when you're out walking and it begins to rain. You usually don't want to get wet, do you? So you pull your clothes around you, tighten up your muscles, sometimes you even screw up your face a bit. You try to keep the rain and all that wetness outside of you.

Carry this experience a bit further. Have you ever found yourself caught in an absolute downpour where there was no escape? At first you tried to stay dry, fighting against the wet. But it soon became hopeless. You could feel the water dripping under your collar. Your shoes started to squish inside. Everything eventually gets absolutely soaked all the way through.

At this point, have you ever thought, "Oh, what the heck!" and deliberately *let go of trying to stay dry?* Then you know what it feels like just to walk in the rain. You relax and sometimes even enjoy it, don't you? You let go! You stop tightening up inside. Your face relaxes.

Now and then you run into people like that on busy streets during a downpour. Everyone else is rushing along, staying tight, and trying to keep the wet out, and here comes this person down the sidewalk with no umbrella, soaked through to the skin, yet sauntering along as if it were a beautiful spring day. You notice such people, don't you? They stand out. They sometimes even make you feel a little angry or envious.

Perhaps they're crazy! That's always a possibility. But there's something in their behavior that you would like to imitate, wouldn't you? Nobody likes to walk around all tense with their face screwed up in a knot. We all want to relax and let go into our environment.

The fourth step in Focusing is something like that. It is letting go into the full, rich felt sense of whatever rises up from within us, not holding it at arm's length or in some way keeping it *outside* our sense of self. There is no tightening up against it, as we usually tighten up against getting wet or getting hurt.

This is just being present in the felt sense, as it is, without trying to figure it out with our heads. It's like being at the beach soaking up the sun or the sound of the waves. We don't hold these outside ourselves. If anything, we enfold them into ourselves, letting them penetrate us. It's like *being in* sports or jogging, where one moves beyond thinking and technique to relishing the sheer physical movement, grace, balance, and inner sense of well-being. We don't *think* sun, waves, or movement. We somehow become them. Letting go into a felt sense is something like that.

We find it helpful in our workshops to have participants recall special moments and memories when they really were *in* some experience without thinking or trying to figure it out. Our approach, then, is to ask: "How was your body during that experience?" "What happened to your mind?" Take a moment right now to recall some such experience yourself.

In response to such questions we have often had people say: "My body felt as though all its pores were open. It was relaxed, floating, still. My mind, though, was *out to lunch!* It just wasn't thinking or trying to figure things out."

By carefully attending to how you are inside during such moments, you can get a better feel for what this step in the Focusing process is all about. The letting go, the being in a felt sense is *beyond* thinking about it. It embraces a bodily knowing that carries awareness inward in a way that thinking can never do.

Have you ever noticed how thinking always remains *outside* of that which is thought? It's the difference between subject and object. We think *about* something. We reason from cause to effect. Even when we think about ourselves, we take a stand outside of that which we think about. That's why reason can never make a tight, hurting inner place unbend! It can't get *inside* it. Solutions in the mind are never the same as a resolution in bodily knowing. Reason always remains *outside* of the hurt that it thinks about. This place may only be entered as the Senoi child was drawn to enter the dream.

Through Focusing, however, a person can finally approach this profound *interiority*. Moving beyond solutions, one finds a realm where *we are carried* more than we carry. We are led as much beyond reason and control as the risk of being inside pain and wetness leads us beyond the way we ordinarily act in our everyday lives. It is like letting go into the challenge of a dream-fall in order to be carried *through* the barrier of forever remaining *outside of our True Self!*

Letting go into a felt sense opens a radically different world within human knowing. Those who risk it experience a kind of neo-Copernican revolution. It's like waking up one morning and knowing for the first time that the sun doesn't go around the earth, even though it looks like it does! It is a shocking, yet liberating discovery.

Letting go into the felt sense marks a point of no return in the Focusing process. It's like crossing a great divide. It's a troublesome point for many, demanding commitment and what can only be called *a believing!* It takes faith to remain in the felt sense, not tampering or fiddling with it, just being there in it until it speaks. If you can do this, you're ready for the fifth and final step in Focusing.

Allowing It to Express Itself. Given time and a faithful remaining in the felt sense without trying to control it or force it in any way, the inner felt meaning will eventually express itself. Sometimes a word or picture will suddenly appear that says

what this is all about. It will often be a spontaneous image. Occasionally there will be tears or an
irrepressible giggling. Some tangible symbol will
eventually arrive, often with a tinge of surprise.

You immediately know the appropriateness or
accuracy of a symbol by the distinct sense of inner
release you feel in your body. This is the *resolution*.
It's an embodied "Yes!" that *always* feels good.
This is the "felt shift" Gendlin has identified. It
occurs in the gifted coming together of symbol
and felt sense within your awareness. The process
moves forward one more step. You sense an inner
movement in your body.

Symbols that arise spontaneously are always
different from those you deliberately think. The
latter are rarely accompanied by any felt shift.
Reason, as we said earlier, remains outside the
hurt, outside the felt sense. But symbols that
apparently come from nowhere, often by surprise,
are usually accompanied by some bodily resolution. The unpredictability makes a difference.

Moreover, the felt shift often brings an inner
release, even though the external problem about
which one is concerned still remains the same.
This points up the paradoxical difference between
solution and resolution. From a therapeutic point
of view, Focusing does not directly solve external
problems. What it can do, however, is support
change in *your body's way of carrying those problems*.

One workshop participant put it well by saying:
"What I'm Focusing on may be painful, but it
always feels good when the right symbol comes

that fits my felt sense." The content may cause distress, but the moving forward of felt meaning, the
resolution in bodily knowing, always brings
release.

This method is not without practical implications for problem solving as well. Whenever a felt
sense is blocked and unable to flow forward,
stress builds up within a person. This stress
siphons away energy and attention from the practical tasks at hand. Concentration diminishes; so
does the capacity for accurate judgment. Focusing
frees a person's resources so he or she can deal
more effectively with the practical decisions
involved in problem solving.

When a blockage can unfold, when the inner
story can be told, tremendous reserves of energy
and attention are made available for other pursuits. Blockage, you know, isn't something that
happens *to* us. *We hold ourselves in a blocked state,*
just as we screw up our faces and hold ourselves
tight in the rain. Blocking is something we do to
ourselves without really wanting to or in any way
knowing how to stop. Yet when we are gifted to
break this cycle and let down our defenses, all the
energy that went into being uptight is now
released.

What usually happens then is that we see things
more clearly. We're able to assess problems more
objectively, and make more accurate judgments.
We don't miss the important things that often slip
by when there's static inside from the burden of

stress that we carry. We become more alert; and this is always a better way to be when trying to solve practical problems.

Carl Rogers once noted that the most accurate scientific instrument available on this planet is the human organism functioning non-defensively in the presence of a problem. Whenever blockage obstructs the forward flow of personhood, there is a corresponding diminishment in our ability to reason and control. So, we find here a very pragmatic reason for regularly putting down the reins. Sometimes we need to lose our lives in order to find them.

When symbol and felt sense come together within the felt shift of bodily knowing, this marks the completion of a single phase in Focusing. Some people stop at this point if resolution has occurred. But most will want to go on further, sensing that this first step is not enough.

The focuser then begins to work with the symbol that felt right and brought a shift. Is it OK to be with this symbol and the new felt sense that accompanied its arrival? If so, a person can move right into Step Four, allowing oneself to be in the feeling of this newness, permitting it gradually to express itself with an additional appropriate symbol. This cycle can be repeated again and again until a natural stopping point is reached.

For example, if you have been Focusing on a vague sense of displeasure at some project of yours that went awry, perhaps the symbol that eventually comes will have something to do with embarrassment. You didn't measure up. You looked bad in the eyes of your friends. That may be true, but something in you still feels that this doesn't quite say it all. You need to go further. So, if it's OK, sit quietly with the felt sense of all that embarrassment, allowing it an opportunity to say what it is. Maybe, after a while, what will come is something about *anger with yourself*. Perhaps that feels more refined, more on target. You're getting closer. If that seems to go far enough, stop. But if you sense that your anger needs to express itself further, then check to see if it would be all right to spend time with this felt sense for a while. Where might it lead you? What tale can it tell in the further unfolding of your self?

Remember that each time a beginner in Focusing decides to go further, he or she should first check to see whether it's OK to go with this new felt sense. If so, just be in it until it eventually expresses itself with some new symbol.

You might think of this inner process as a chain. Each link that completes one cycle serves as a point of connection and starting point for the next. Perhaps imagining an onion coming apart one layer at a time will help you picture this process.

It's good to point out, as Gendlin does, that no single shift in the felt sense is an absolute answer to anything. Each individual movement must always be situated within a broader pattern.

In focusing you will often find that some words, which come with a strong sense of righteousness at a given moment and give you a body shift, are later superseded by what comes at a later step. You cannot—and should not—trust any *single* set of words, any *one* feeling, any *one* body message that comes. But you can definitely trust the whole series of steps by which your body moves to resolve and change a wrong state of being. You can trust that, even if the words and understanding of a given step are superseded, that step was the right step to come then, at that moment, and will lead to the right next step from there.[2]

Trust the overall pattern, therefore. The message is the process and the process is the message.

This very gentle, non-manipulative procedure is what Focusing is all about. There are variations, some of which were developed by colleagues of Dr. Gendlin. There are instructions about what to do if one gets stuck or can't get hold of a felt sense. Many strategies are suggested for maintaining contact with felt meaning as well as what to do if it should slip away and be lost. All this is fine and helpful insofar as learning *a technique* is concerned.

But the challenging bio-spiritual dimension of this experience is that *no matter how carefully one follows any of these directions, their exact observance can in no way make something happen!* They are powerless to *effect* the very change toward which Focusing is aimed. This is the surprise and challenge one experiences after Focusing over a period of time.

Careful adherence to the instructions for Focusing does not *make* anything happen. All it can do is insure that a person will be more or less situated within the realm of inner experiencing where change *can* and *may* occur. It *positions us* for the possibility of bodily resolution. But if there is to be transformation of any sort, *a radically different, non-voluntary and apparently gratuitous element must then take over.* This subtle new dynamic seeks its own direction, measures its own rhythm, and flows totally beyond the voluntary process that brought the focuser to the initial point of contact in the first place.

Following the directions for Focusing is much like paddling a canoe from some protected inlet out into the middle of a river. Once there, several things can happen. Sometimes you paddle deliberately into a current. Sometimes, the flow of the river catches you unaware, bearing you along in its grasp. Sometimes you just paddle around and go nowhere. Nothing happens. Following the instructions can only get you out into the middle of your own inner stream. Once there, you soon discover that the stream has a life and movement of its own. *It does not bend to your paddling any more than your canoe can change the course of the river's flow.* All you can do is go with it in case it should catch you and carry you along.

The bio-spiritual challenge involves a delicate balance between purposeful striving and then letting go of the reins. It is a matter of knowing where to be, and then being there with an attitude of patient expectation. It calls for disciplined preparation, but then *allowing* time and space for a deeper knowing and a process to manifest itself.

Focusing supports this bio-spiritual perspective. There lies within each of us a surprise of grace that can arrive within bodily knowing. There is an inner movement beyond all control whose remote horizon seems to be well beyond the passing concerns of everyday survival.

A cosmic story unfolds in each of us. Couched in the language of bodily knowing, it passes largely unnoticed beneath the stream of daily awareness. It conveys a deeper message shrouded in this still early dawn of consciousness evolution. We are as yet only dimly aware of ourselves— each is a flickering point of brightness that fades off into regions of darker unknowing.

3

Why we teach Focusing
in the context of spirituality

Sometimes we hear the comment that Focusing is
primarily a therapeutic tool best used to get one's
house in order as a preparation for meditation and
spiritual searching. We wish to share our reserva-
tions about this view because we in no way limit
Focusing to this more obvious therapeutic role.

Focusing, we believe, is far more integrative
and comprehensive in its psychological dynamics.
In one simple experience it unites the benefits of
psychophysical therapy with meditation's emphasis on centering, active receptivity, and expanded
awareness. Moreover, all this is realized in a per-
sonally tailored, developmental fashion according
to the rhythm and ability of each person to inte-
grate this step into their lives. We see no reason to
limit Focusing to problem solving, crisis intervention, or just the preparation for meditation—
although all these uses are certainly valid.

We feel that Focusing offers a developmental
approach to some of the most basic elements of
meditation. Wherever the focuser happens to be in
their spiritual development, he or she is plunged

directly into two essential ingredients of meditation: an initial striving or preparatory aspect, and then the alert waiting and receptivity that are so often rewarded with an eventual shift in consciousness.

Focusing teaches a marvelous balance because it integrates these two essential elements of personal and spiritual growth. It can create a posture, a presence, eventually even a lifestyle of "caring detachment" so difficult to realize in our competitive, control-oriented society. The integrative nature of Focusing somehow reconciles the apparent opposites of "caring" and "detachment" into a higher level synthesis within the focuser. This synthesis manifests itself most profoundly in the maturing quality of presence with which one can live one's ordinary life.

In this chapter we would like to show how Focusing can address three critical issues in spirituality.

1. The perennial problem of "getting out of the mind"
2. The challenge of being drawn into an awareness of some Larger Process
3. How one's own "body knowing" is a key to forward movement in these two areas

What do we mean by *mind?* The word is used in many ways within different spiritual traditions. We use it here in a limited sense that refers to the rational, linear thinking process. It is a way of identifying all the chatter in the skull associated with analyzing, planning, and problem solving.

Our own search for a psychologically healthy spirituality has led both of us to conclude that getting out of the mind is really allowing one's self to be drawn more fully into body knowing. *You get out of the mind by getting into the body.* These are not separate or distinct activities. Moreover, body knowing provides the immediate, practical framework within which spiritual awareness is apparently meant to function.

Human evolution is rooted in an "embodied" person, and "higher level consciousness" involves an unfolding of the entire person. Although such a fundamental realization appears to be part of every wisdom tradition, it is also something that various expressions of this tradition in religion and spirituality have often lost or neglected. This is certainly the case within Christianity today. Realizing that a more holistic, process-oriented, bio-spirituality was needed to support a *felt sense* for having one's being within some greater Mystery, we have been drawn to Focusing.

There are two critical issues in spiritual development as far as we are concerned. The first is to discover a holistic approach for letting go of the mind's omnipotent control as a prelude to allowing some broader wisdom within the entire human organism to speak. The second is to allow the unique next step that is *me* to emerge as an integral, harmonious expression of some Larger Process.

For centuries various spiritual traditions have identified a blocking experience of the mind as *the* central issue in spiritual growth. The problem of seeking to use the finely honed power of reason to control everything in one's life seems to be the primary issue faced by anyone serious about spiritual growth. The omnipotence that we grant to the power of intellect becomes our downfall. This magnificent potential of reason was never meant to be a tool with which to control absolutely everything that touches human existence.

Yet we all balk at the risk involved in setting aside the very means by which we are accustomed to survive. We cherish our ability to "think out" and "solve" problems, and rightfully so. But the tendency to vest so much of our personal identity in an exercise of reason and control can deafen us to the inviting call and surrender to some greater meaning and purpose in life.

One soon discovers at the threshold of spiritual awareness an interwoven web of uniquely personal fears. We are reluctant to let go of the security we create with our wits. We are afraid of losing our more or less familiar self-identity. This is a familiar scenario for any maturing human being, as well as for those engaged in the helping professions and for spiritual counselors.

It is incredible how our ambitions, dreams, hopes, and fears, even our deepest longings for peace and justice can often confuse and sidetrack us from concentrating our attention on this central issue. We find so many sincere, well-intentioned people who continually fall into the trap of living as though ideals could be actualized by better *understanding* them, preaching them, researching or analyzing them, discussing or organizing them into rules and regulations. Some become so involved in this monumental effort that like the king and his mesmerized followers they are unable to see that everyone is naked and things simply are not working. It is a difficult lesson for idealists as well as for generous and dedicated religious activists to learn. Ideals, praiseworthy goals, morals, ethics, religious values, worship—all are just as open to misuse as any so-called worldly pursuit. These, too, can become a hindrance to letting go of the mind's instinctive tendency to control everything.

Whenever someone falls under the spell of using methods of control in order to achieve spiritual ideals or religious goals, such values and altruistic pursuits, praiseworthy in themselves, can become obstacles. They blind a person to the very direction and answers that may be sought within the benevolence and grace of the Cosmos. We have found that Focusing provides a practical framework within which trust can grow. It is a trust that gradually makes possible the actual living of what our ideals represent.

We also find that Focusing can support spiritual growth by inviting a person to step beyond the mind's perpetual quest for control. It provides a practical framework for encouraging that "art of allowing" within which we can gently be taught to trust a deeper bodily-felt wisdom. Focusing has an uncanny way of keeping a person on the right track. It constantly surfaces the pivotal, personal issues that provide an immediate point of entry into bodily knowing. By its very nature, therefore, Focusing creates the right climate for spirituality.

While Focusing, one does not introduce any of the more traditional approaches used to gain meditative attention. One sets aside prayerful considerations—the reading of scriptures, using a mantrum, mandala or koan, the Jesus Prayer, one's own breathing, or any other physical action like dance or aikido. These activities do not necessarily center attention on, nor express the unique next step of unfolding that is proper to the one who focuses—so, they are not used.

Rather, Focusing brings attention as well as receptivity to bear on what the focuser allows his or her body to indicate has first priority in life right now. Something uniquely personal that *feels* like it is important enough to be more fully aware of one's entire being.

The particular value of Focusing, when used in a spiritual context, lies in the way it opens a door beyond thinking and control. Instead of programmed input or activity that may be used to draw attention beyond the mind, Focusing allows a bodily-felt sense for the next step in life to form and provide the practical framework within which meditative attention is realized. In a single act, the focuser is drawn out of the mind and into the body. But the body side of this equation is one that, as we shall see in a moment, is a potentially fruitful interface between ego's concern for control and an inrush of grace from the Cosmos.

What we have in Focusing, then, is a setting for sound spirituality that is simultaneously realized within a context of sound psychology.

In our culture it is difficult to judge accurately the contribution of religion and the various spiritual disciplines. What elements in them actually contribute to healthy human development and what, instead, cause harm? Trying to sort this out is like stumbling through a booby-trapped field. It's so easy to step into the wrong place and get blown off the path of your own inner wisdom. We can easily be beguiled by the promises and rewards of this or that spiritual path.

People long today as always for personal meaning, security, and connectedness. They seek ethical and moral guidelines for a better understanding of the "why's" and "what's" of life. In an age that is characterized by the absence of such guidelines, people welcome almost any attempt to respond to this vacuum. Such vulnerability, though, gives rise to a naïveté and a hiatus in critical perception where few people realize that the way they use religion *is actually part of the problem* of blocked change and growth, not the solution. Entire communities and groups of religious or spiritually oriented people become thwarted in this fashion. They pass on a kind of blindness from generation to generation, all in the name of God, religion, or enlightenment of some kind or another.

Focusing brings a badly needed freshness and honesty into all of this. One of our workshop participants tried to describe something of her experience in a recent letter. She wrote:

Focusing reaches the inner knowing and bypasses the outer beliefs. The Spirit knows when things are not "right" at the deepest level, when the intellect can only guess at the cause, and not always accurately, most times preventing those "felt shifts" wherein the real cause starts to dissipate. It is healing from the inside-out, affording the human mind little chance for self-deception.

Another person wrote:

There can be so much self-deception in a talking-to-God kind of prayer. Focusing, though, helps me to put my body and all that's there (hurting, scary, or otherwise) where my good intentions are in prayer. I can't use talking to God as an escape from being in touch with the truth of myself. One must let go of the controlling mind and all its chatter, let go into what the body knows. Otherwise, you can't focus. It puts my trust in God, my faith in Divine Providence right on the line! I have to risk letting the answers come as they will, not make them up myself. Focusing invites me *actually to believe with my*

body, not just my mind. It invites me to live
my faith in a benevolent, loving Providence
as a whole person.

Statements such as these reveal the journey
inward. They come like letters from a distant traveler walking some risky byway beyond the mind's
control. A good novelist or biographer can never
really catch the meanings, the deeper dimensions,
or connectedness of people's lives without somehow "getting inside" the skin of his or her subject.
So too, each of us is meant to be drawn inside to
touch the marvelous, unique story that is ourselves.

The psychological dynamics of Focusing encourage us to *allow symbols to happen.* Such symbols can
teach us to wait patiently before the awesome
Mystery of humankind, a mystery hidden within
the story in our own bodies. Being on the right path
to discover this message seems to hinge on whether
we learn to allow that story of The Whole which is
in us, to appear. When the symbol comes unbidden, when the surprise of a new direction unfolds
within our bodily knowing, we realize what it is to
be drawn beyond the mind. We also sense at the
same time a benevolent process that carries us
beyond our limited, control-oriented selves.

There is a story in time and human history
unfolding in each of us. It is a story with roots, a
cosmic tied-in-ness and pattern of meaning not
bounded by the limitations of our particular
moment in history. But to open even the first

chapter, let alone continue reading until the glimmer of some Larger Pattern and rootedness begin
to emerge, involves getting inside our bodies in a
special way. This, it seems, is the key message
contained within the perennial spiritual traditions of the world. And this is where we feel
Focusing can make an exciting and significant
contribution.

The Kingdom of Heaven is within! Our individual stories, which are integral to the entire Cosmic
narrative, are written in our bodies. Any approach
to spirituality that neglects or tries to bypass this
blunt bio-spiritual fact is ultimately dead-ended
and off the track of human evolution.

Some people write today about having "recov-
ered their bodies and feelings" as though this were
an accomplished fact and now they can go on to
something else. Others strive through "spiritual"
practices to transcend both body and feelings. The
two of us believe that the story we are meant to
write with our lives is one that continues to unfold,
but not within some disembodied center of awareness. It blossoms forth within a bodily-felt sense
that *is* consciousness-potential itself.

"Recovering our bodies" is really the lifelong
process of allowing the knowing-potential of the
entire organism to open, thereby revealing an
underlying plot of unity hidden between the lines
of what appears as a disconnected narrative.
Whenever a felt sense unfolds, whenever a symbol appears from beyond the narrowed edge of
reason and control, then we can catch sight of the

Larger Mystery written within the story that is ourselves. We can begin to trust. Perhaps more important, we may discover a gifted believing that is written in our bodies.

Each experience of *felt shift* opens an extraordinary window on a vast, largely unexplored world of human awareness. It is a realm of tangible *connection*. A place from which to touch and taste with bodily knowing. Beyond every rationalization and mental construct, here at last one finds the body's inward lookout point on an expanding universe.

Given the cultural heritage of most Westerners today, we believe Focusing has a potential for becoming, perhaps, the most important ingredient in a lifestyle that we would call spiritual. Spiritual, in the sense that this mode of self-awareness called Focusing provides a structure within which one can bring the consciousness-potential of the whole organism within the scope of some Larger Cosmic Process.

4

Humor, playfulness, and surprise

The vulnerability of ego

Focusing is full of surprises, and the unexpected occurs quite often. One session in particular stands out for the two of us. Ed had experienced a painful, somewhat foreboding felt sense. It was quite uncomfortable for him. Together we tried various approaches, hoping the right symbol might break through to awareness; but all to no avail. The effort seemed futile until suddenly Ed had a tremendous urge to giggle. It was an infectious inner tickling that could not be contained. We both found it a relief to laugh, and we shared our amusement at something neither of us could fully comprehend. Then, in the midst of this hilarity, the dark cloud of a felt sense suddenly poked its head around some inner psychic corner and shouted, "Boo!" Immediately and spontaneously the image of a laughing Buddha appeared; it was seated in a lotus position with hands raised in the air merrily laughing.

At this point there was a distinct felt shift. The inner landscape became totally transformed. The felt sense was entirely different. Yet the foreboding aspect of inner meaning had not been symbolized as we had expected. Nevertheless, despite its initial, somewhat ominous expression, the inner felt sense was now no longer an enemy. A kind of gentle amusement, even playfulness, appeared once the felt sense had been owned and accepted.

The flavor of this experience remained for several days. It was totally unexpected, and we enjoyed talking about its implications. More than anything else, the spontaneous upsurge of humor and lightheartedness piqued our curiosity. We were charmed by the element of surprise.

There is a comfortable predictability about reason. Maybe that's why it has never been thought of as the royal road of spiritual advancement. Reason can never comprehend the miraculous, the unpredictable, the larger pattern. In the narrowed world of control there is little room for playfulness and surprise. Indeed, surprise is the enemy! *Yet availability for surprise is a necessary disposition for growth in the spiritual life.*

An example of just such a surprise came during one of Pete's Focusing sessions a few years ago. We'll keep our narrative in the first person to preserve the flavor of this unique experience. Pete's story unfolds as follows:

It was a distressing time for me. A recurring bout of severe lower back spasms associated with a cracked vertebra had kept me in bed for over a week. Along with the physical pain, I was also trying to cope with mounting fear and depression. Catastrophic expectations loomed large in my awareness as I chafed at my immobility and the unpredictable nature of what I was experiencing. How soon might this happen again? How long would it last? The slightest twinge of pain pushed me toward preoccupation with self and defensive isolation. Presence to anything other than my own panic and concern was practically impossible.

Talking to myself did no good. Praying was hopeless. No amount of reasoning was able to break through my brooding sense of fear and depression. It just wouldn't let go! I felt divided against myself. All of me that wanted to live and move with ease and freedom felt squeezed into the upper part of my head and shoulders, as though trying to shrink as far away as possible from the pain in my lower back.

I desperately wanted direction in all of this confusion. I not only wanted meaning, but also some way of *growing through* rather than simply *enduring* this experience. I needed to be in my pain and my frustrated feeling of dependence in a different way. So I used Focusing to draw near to all my depression, helplessness, and the terrifying possibilities I had conjured up for myself. Instead of seeking a direction from *outside* my fear, I finally decided to walk the inner road to see what might happen.

The image which eventually came surprised me. It was far more profound than I realized at first. It was a response that answered my problem by restating the question. There was a distinct body sense to the imagery. It felt right.

A new perspective was born. The image helped me walk *through* pain to a broadened vista on life and myself. It was as though I could actually feel myself being drawn to some larger picture. The knowing which I experienced in that brief moment was a realizing of the way *through* my fear and confusion. *That in itself was the answer!* Not an answer *to* fear, but a way of being *in* fear or any feeling, positive or negative, which might allow the unveiling of some deeper bio-spiritual perspective.

The image came in a flash, from the midst of pain and confusion. It came unbidden with no prior consideration on my part. It was the memory of an incident I had not recalled for almost forty years. A trivial event. Yet, now it returned with meaning and a power that caught me by surprise. It made a connection! And in that connection I was blessed with the first of a long series of bodily-felt releases from fear and tension. What, then, was the image?

As a youngster I had, for health reasons, attended a boarding school in the Arizona desert. It was an isolated little ranch about twenty miles from Tucson. Horseback riding was available, and I soon fell in love with getting out on a mount and riding for miles through the desert.

We weren't allowed to do this alone, of course. But one morning at dawn, when I was only seven years old, I used the watering trough to stand on and saddled up alone before any staff or children were stirring. Then I rode straight out into the sunrise. It was a glorious day and I explored the desert for an hour or more, giving little thought to anything except what lay ahead of me. At some point it dawned on me to get my bearings, and I turned to check for familiar landmarks. But the surrounding arroyos gave no hint of a direction home. There were no familiar markers. No paths or trails. Just sagebrush, cactus, and an unending series of little hills that all looked the same. I realized with a sudden chill that I was lost!

Searching for a while, I desperately tried to find my way home, but I soon realized it was hopeless. I remember my inner panic and growing sense of isolation—much like feelings that would come in later life whenever fear or confusion would overtake me. Only gradually did my attention return to my horse, who was peacefully waiting for me to signal with reins and stirrups where we were to go next.

At that point I was inspired to do one of the few sensible things a youngster in my predicament could do. I stopped trying to figure things out for myself and made what may have been one of the first consciously deliberate acts of trust in my young life. I knew I was lost, but deep down I felt that *the horse knew his way home!* The remembered experience of how I deliberately lifted the reins and let them drop on the horse's neck somehow fit what my body knew about pain and confusion as I focused forty years later. It had not been forgotten!

There had been a deliberate letting go and trusting out there in the desert years before. It was a letting go of everything that wanted to control the situation, a kind of abandonment to some wisdom that lay beyond anything I could muster within myself.

That morning among the sage brush and cacti, the horse's first response to my loosening of the reins was to begin nibbling the sparse grass at his feet. I didn't urge him anywhere but just left the reins loose and waited. Unaccustomed to such lack of direction, he stood still for a while looking about before he moved to get more grass.

I recall wondering how long it would take him to get the point. I didn't know my way back to the ranch and had no way of communicating this to the horse. It would take time for him to realize that I had voluntarily become a bundle of inert baggage that he could carry anywhere he wished.

I remember how hard it was to resist the temptation to move him about. I desperately wanted to reassert my control, holding the reins, guiding him now one way, now another. But my feeling, even as a child, was that he had to experience a sense of himself as boss if we were ever to get home before nightfall. And so I waited . . . and waited . . . and waited. It seemed endless.

Finally I noticed the horse stretching his neck, shaking his head, and testing the looseness of the reins. Instead of grazing haphazardly, he began to move in a definite direction. Snatching mouthfuls of grass, he would move on a few paces before reaching for another tuft as we passed.

Gradually the stops became less frequent, his pace quickened, and eventually he broke into a trot, with only occasional questioning looks over his shoulder, and then a determined, careening gallop. Ahead lay oats, the corral, and getting this infernal saddle off his back—not to mention the young rider hanging on for dear life.

It was a wild ride home; I narrowly missed the outstretched spines of cholla cactus and barely grazed the giant saguaro so plentiful in that part of the desert. Terrified, I clutched the saddle horn, torn between a desperate desire to rein in this lurching juggernaut and the equally strong fear that if I did we might never get home.

Finally familiar landmarks appeared. We slowed, stopped, and rested a bit. I even imagined a mischievous glint in the equine eye as he turned to see how I was doing.

The rest of the return was uneventful. Little did I then realize that the personal significance of this event would lie dormant in me for almost forty years before coming back to teach me more about myself.

I have learned through Focusing that the way home is written deep within each of us. Somewhere beneath all of our daily *reacting*—getting jobs done, meals prepared, bills paid, and all our survival planning—lies a realm of deeper meaning, purpose, and direction. The horse, as I have found through Focusing, is really a largely unowned aspect of ourselves. There is something within each of us that knows the real meaning of human life. At certain times it can break through the shallow awareness that fills most of our waking moments.

What I want to say is that during the Focusing episode I am presently describing, my pain, fear, depression, and helplessness in that instant came to be for me like the horse. Instead of seeking to ride these feelings in a controlling way, I realized what was needed was for me to be with/in them in a different manner.

When I hold the reins, it *feels differently* than when I let them fall. I'm speaking not only physically but psychologically. When you are in control, everything comes to you as to a spider at the center of its web. Control means readiness to react. Being on top of the survival game.

Letting go of the reins is more like *being carried*. It is a different psychological stance, a different physical feeling. Your center somehow changes; it becomes less precise and broader in scope. It *includes* more! You feel and respond out of something bigger than your ability to control.

That, for me, is the beginning of bio-spiritual awareness! It is finding a way through to some larger *At-Homeness* written deep within bodily knowing. There is wisdom in the horse, and the horse is *us!*

I believe this is why that image from childhood means so much to me. It helped me to realize that fear and helplessness are a special doorway into a more profound realm of what my life is all about. I found an encouraging sign that I was on the right track.

I didn't gain control over fear. Rather, I discovered a bodily-felt way of being in fear so it could draw me into the mystery of some farther horizon. I didn't *solve* problems so much as *gain a new perspective*. The surprising thing, though, was how that change of perspective affected my body! I could *feel* the tightness of fear begin to unbend. Yet I had no control over what was happening. I was not *doing* something. It was doing itself.

There is so much mystery in bodily knowing. It doesn't follow the dictates of reason. One finds, instead, a world of wisdom and surprise that can only be entered in a very special way. As the cowboys of old had to check their guns at the barroom door, we too must first lay down the overriding need to control all of our lives before we cross the threshold of bio-spiritual journeying.

Each of us must learn our own personal language of transcendence. There is a difference between *solutions* that we think out in our minds, and a gifted *resolution* in a way our bodies carry issues and problems. Playfulness and surprise often accompany this graced inner release. We are drawn beyond the narrow scope of reason into some greater sense for ourselves. There is vastness within. There is a vital cosmic connection that lies on the edge of human awareness.

Just writing these words, now, calls up a felt sense. The reserve of bodily knowing rushes in to say "Yes" in its own inimitable fashion.

We recall a short vacation we had in Montreal during the World's Fair—Expo '67. It was a day of sharp contrasts as we visited the Soviet and British pavilions one right after the other. A certain heaviness hung over the Russian exhibit with its excessive emphasis on productivity. The goal of several Five Year Plans had either been achieved or surpassed. Technical competence and achievements

in space—all were there and were of great importance to the Soviets. One could not help being
impressed. Yet after a time it became tiring.

Outside the pavilion the sun was shining as we
strolled over to the next exhibit. What a surprise!
Upon entering the British pavilion we were led
through a series of clever exhibits in which the
British poked gentle fun at their own foibles and
idiosyncrasies, as only the British can do. It was a
delightful journey that brought a refreshing inner
lightness. Toward the end we were led through a
twisting, tunnel-like enclosure that abruptly
opened out to a large room filled with immense El
Greco-like figures by Giacometti, their arms
extended skyward. The experience brought goose
pimples. There was a sense of movement, a
breadth of vision. The long sweep of transcendence had burst forth like a natural conclusion
to the humor and playfulness that preceded
it. Everything was so right! It fit. It hung together,
and we felt we were at the edge of something
very great.

We walked beneath these towering figures for a
bit, like miniature wanderers through a gigantic
frozen ballet. And then we left. But the memory
has remained, and it returns now like some forgotten melody to add a richer texture to the current
unfolding of our lives.

Humor and playfulness are somehow part of
transcendence. They are one more way the human
person says "Yes" to being within some greater

reality. They are an unrationalized, organismic admission that the limited center and sense of self are *not* the total picture. In such experiences one catches a glimpse of growing comfortableness with going beyond the familiar, the habitual, and the structure-bound. It's OK to have limitations, not to know all the answers, not to have everything under control.

Focusing opens the possibility for such surprises within bodily knowing. It reveals inner movements much like a mountain stream that keeps on inviting you around some enchanting next bend.

But there is a darker side to all this as well, an unsettling reluctance to face the nightmare. *Resistance!* This, too, colors our experience of transcendence. There is humor, lightness, challenge, and surprise. But there is also the reluctance to take the next step.

Let's consider the disquieting nature of this bio-spiritual journey. What perceived risks cause us to hesitate? Why do we so often feel an inner tension at what this venture may demand from us? Can we, perhaps, find direction for ourselves right within the reluctant foot-dragging that frequently characterizes our first halting steps into this realm of bodily knowing?

There is an unsettling dimension to the bio-spiritual enterprise. We inevitably hesitate at the start, hanging back from the risks of this hazardous venture. We resist letting go into organismic awareness not only because reason protests that it is often unreliable. There is also the far more disturbing call to step beyond the very familiarity of reason itself.

Unreliability we can somehow cope with. It's the vulnerability we cannot stand! Letting go into a felt sense means letting go of reason's control.

Spiritual teachers as well as the wisdom literature of many religious traditions have all explored this hanging back from taking the next step. Such resistance, though, is actually a blessing in disguise because it teaches us so much about ourselves. It is never in itself a block to bio-spiritual progress! Like the nightmare, it can be a marvelous teacher, a wonderful guide, an avenue of entry into the miraculous.

The term *ego* is often used in this context. Like other words it has many meanings. The two of us are not interested in listing these meanings here. We would like, however, to share what this word has come to mean for us. We identify *ego* as the entire experience associated with trying to be in control. All our survival efforts, the activity of reason, our identity associated with this manner of knowing—all this, for us, is ego.

Hopefully, you can conclude from this that ego is never something to be gotten rid of. Without it you couldn't survive. Yet it needs to be located properly in the broader framework of a more complete human life. As in Focusing, there are times for deliberate effort, for paddling your canoe. Then there are times for setting such striving aside. But even when doing this, ego is never completely abandoned. The bud is always in the flower, but the flower is always *more than* the bud. At this point one simply waits to be called farther forward, if that is to happen. It is a moment of potentially tangible transcendence. It is being touched by grace.

You might think of the caterpillar; how busy it is. With a magnifying glass you can be amazed by the spectacle of its survival activity as it chews a path along the edge of a luscious leaf. You behold the dynamic synthesis of organic matter into organic matter. There is a deliberate, sometimes frenzied effort to gorge as much food as possible into this little creature.

But then comes the slowing down, a quieting, a period of greater attending within. Now deeper forces take over. No longer the passionate quest for gratification. Instead, a cocoon of stillness. Then it happens. Metamorphosis!

Ego is like the caterpillar—an exciting place of beginning and transformation. It is an apt image of our Body of Flesh within which, one day, there can arise a magnificent dawning of Spirit.

But what of our own metamorphosis? Where can we begin? Perhaps, like the Senoi child in a dream, we will discover the deeper place of Spirit by starting with our own nightmare—the current resistance that holds us back from further unfolding.

It's interesting and instructive to discover the various patterns of ego defense a person may build up against getting more involved with their bodily knowing. Sometimes these defenses are subtle and can be quite funny. Pete, for example, used to find when beginning to Focus that he was confronted almost immediately by the same recurring theme. After only a moment of trying to be in the felt sense, an identical pattern of resistance would appear. *It was the list of jobs he still had to do around the house and in the office!* Again and again this list would appear and Pete would be led into considering the various items it contained, planning which of them he would do next, what tools were needed, what purchases had to be made, and so on.

In the beginning we thought of the list as a major distraction and its regular appearance was greeted with considerable annoyance. But before long the real significance became obvious. During one Focusing session Ed made the suggestion: "How does always having this list of things to do feel in your body right now? Why not just focus on that?" The suggestion was not meant to get Pete involved with thinking *about* the various items on the list. Rather, he was simply invited to attend more carefully to the inner sense of this image, allowing the feeling of it to unfold.

This particular Focusing episode led the two of us on a long and interesting journey. We got into many things, primarily the need we have for control and the fear of losing control. We journeyed together through the intense satisfaction that comes from getting jobs done. Crossing things off the list! We then sat with the anxiety of situations where tasks never seemed to be completed, where there were too many loose ends. In each instance what we touched was not the unique content of some item that could be thought about. Rather, it was an opportunity to *be in* the unfinishedness of the task, the loss of control, the good feeling of completing a project, and the felt meaning of all this.

In an amazing way, this initial resistance proved to be the best possible avenue of entry into the Focusing process. The experience has been repeated again and again in workshops and counseling sessions with others. The resistance that most severely blocks letting go into bodily knowing provides a priceless point of entry into the further story of felt meaning within each of us. No matter what the resistance—fatigue, being overwhelmed by it all, a sense that all this is silly, terror at what might be discovered, feeling embarrassed, not wanting to take up so much of other people's time, feeling uncomfortable because I can't find any problem to focus on, feeling blank and at an inner standstill, being bored—all these resistances and many more have turned into valuable doorways and marvelous beginnings.

Any hanging back from your painful felt sense is *always* a sign of hope! If this seems strange, remember that right within the resistance itself you can discover another loose thread leading into the tapestry of bodily knowing. Whenever pain is too much to bear, whenever knocking at the front door of a troublesome felt sense requires more courage than you can muster, there is always a side entrance, a cellar window, some unnoticed opening through which to gain entry.

Recall Step Three in the Focusing process, checking whether it's OK to be with a felt sense. When the answer is "No," this does not mean everything comes to a crashing halt. You have an alternative. Instead of taking your difficult felt sense head on, you ask whether it would be all right to spend time with the repugnance, fear, or apprehension that lies behind your "No." You turn *to the resistance itself* as your next best opening into what needs to be focused upon.

Hope, then, lies in the very hanging back through which you shun involvement with bodily knowing. There is a feeling edge in such resistance. It is real. Tangible. Accessible. An alternate path along which to be drawn toward your next forward step. It's not always easy. But neither does it leave you hopelessly mired in the dead end of your own depression and discouragement. There is never any circumstance within which you can't find some doorway of growth.

We frequently wonder about this apparent paradox. Why does inner resistance and defensiveness so often provide the best port of entry into bodily knowing? Why should nightmares pave a way toward the birth of some new inner creation? It's so strange. Mysterious. Teilhard de Chardin closed his epic work, *The Phenomenon of Man*, with this searching final reflection: "In one manner or the

other it still remains true that, even in the view of
the mere biologist, the human epic resembles nothing so much as a way of the Cross." [1]

Survival means strengthening the ego and
extending the refinement of control. Evolution, on
the other hand, means gambling all on the possibility of being drawn farther forward in the
unfolding of our own story. Crucifixion lies not in
the goal toward which we are carried. That is a joy.
A bodily resurrection! It's in the *letting go* of security associated with what we already know that is
so painful. That's what we feel in such resistance.
It is the challenge of believing. We must first
mature beyond ego-perception before we are
drawn into the unfolding of a more integral and
lasting Self.

Survival, of course, is absolutely necessary if
evolution is to succeed. But the perspective of ego
is so narrow. It lacks depth; human depth. The
approach to everything is so limited. Always seeing from the outside. Calculating. Manipulating.
Predicting. Controlling. What needs to be abandoned are not these fine survival skills but the
sense for ourselves that has become totally identified with this narrower perspective.

But how can this occur? Is it something we
deliberately *do* for ourselves—setting out to divest
ourselves of ego? The two of us don't think so.

Michael Murphy once wrote a marvelously
speculative story about an enthralling experiment
on the leading edge of human evolution. It
includes intriguing references to Einstein-Rosen

bridges, mind-holes, DNA molecules, and passages to other worlds. The principal character in this fascinating enterprise is a young man whose name provides the title for the book, *Jacob Atabet*.[2] Jacob attempts to journey into the farther reaches of human consciousness. Expanding awareness into both microcosm and macrocosm is the goal of his heroic adventure.

Jacob Atabet is consumed by a burning desire to discover how individual awareness can ultimately break through to cosmic consciousness. How can a person transcend the limitations of ego and the individual sensory world? For Jacob, the question is simple enough: Is it possible to change the rules of what he calls "the body game?"

In his pursuit of an answer, Jacob seeks a hidden formula through which by personal effort he may transcend the limits of reason and ego-awareness. Practicing what he regards as an evolutionary asceticism, he strives by sheer acts of the will to reach beyond the limited knowing potential of his own organism into the embrace of some wider consciousness. In the end, Jacob Atabet nearly destroys himself, finally realizing that there are no shortcuts.

Michael Murphy's story recounts a fictional attempt to reach past the boundaries of ego. In order for this to happen there must be changes in the rules of the body-game. *But can we make such changes by ourselves?*

We think not. Effort there must be, but effort of a different sort. Not a straining to evolve, but a constant, disciplined faithfulness to our own advancing story. We do not change the rules. *The rules are changed for us!*

Jacob Atabet, we feel, tragically missed the mark. Being drawn beyond ego is not something that is wrested from the universe like some prized mineral that is arduously dug from the earth. Rather, *it is given to us,* as butterfly wings emerge from the caterpillar when the time is ripe.

The question of ego-transcendence, then, is not some esoteric adventure, a striving to achieve an altered state of consciousness. Neither is it an asceticism of willpower and control. True enlightenment appears to be nothing more *nor less* than taking your own next step, *allowing* a process to go forward.

The fruits of successful Focusing are never forced to the surface by personal effort. You cannot deliberately set out to change something through Focusing. The change is gift. Grace. The inner struggle is not one of willpower, trying to *make something happen.* Rather, the effort involved is in remaining faithful to your own deeper story, believing in the *depth* of yourself. Taking up the daily cross of being in each resistance that holds you back from letting go into your next step forward.

The prophet Isaiah records a powerful and compelling image for the Hebrew people. In it the God of Israel speaks a message that echoes down through the centuries. It brings strength and guidance to many people who follow the Judeo-Christian path.

When you pass through the waters
   I will be with you;
when you walk through fire
   you shall not be burned,
and the flame shall not consume you.
         (Isa. 43:2 RSV)

An enduring Presence animates the history and the wandering of those who have been nourished by this Old Testament tradition.

But apply these words of the prophet to your own inner world. There is a remarkable parallel with the unfolding of inner life. The felt sense can be a place of fire and flood, confusion, turbulence, and pain. It is beyond control, beyond the crafted security that ego can provide.

A call into the desert drew the Hebrews from their familiar Egyptian landscape into the untamed wilderness of Sinai. What they lived as an external, historical event we experience today in the unfolding of our own inner sense of self. Focusing provides an Exodus context for each of us. It places us in the wilderness area of our own open-ended journey, our pilgrimage, our wandering in the realm of evolutionary surprise.

This is a desert place for most of us because we usually come to know ourselves as ego, as the ones who strive for control. Yet here, control must be abandoned in favor of a new way of being.

Two vital experiences happened to the Israelites during their Exodus wandering, two experiences that radically transformed their sense of themselves. They discovered a new identity, and in it they were touched by the saving power of God.

The desert was beyond all control, yet out of this strange wilderness came wonders and surprise. Water gushed forth from a rock. Manna fell from above. They were given a cloud by day and a pillar of fire by night to guide them.

The Israelites heard a voice that spoke to them in this wilderness, a voice from beyond the habitual, the familiar, the secure. The protective shell of their hardened ego was blistered by the desert sun—cracked, broken, and eventually transformed. Exodus for the Israelites was a time of conversion. Beyond all their resistance a new identity lay waiting to be born. They were to discover themselves as gift, as graced. They would find within the limitations of their own flesh the seed of God.

So, too, with each one of us in our time. What Hebrew could imagine the surprise of living water gushing forth from an arid desert rock? Who among us can imagine that the hard place of inner resistance—anger, frustration, fear, and confusion— might one day open up to point the way home?

Do we yet know the gift that we are? Have we explored that inner reserve beyond our ego?

Exodus is now. It is the story of Everyman, Everywoman, and Everychild. It is a journey lived over and over again. It is the commitment to a greater depth of humanness. It is finding in life much more than simply the will to survive. It is testing the waters of deeper identity. Being drawn beyond all willing into the embrace of a wider bio-spiritual quest.

5

Restoring inner process

The evolution of God consciousness

Have you ever experienced moments of quiet in which you suddenly realized your life has become little more than a series of *reactions* to one crisis after another? As each of us grows older, we long to live more of each remaining day not like a cork bobbing up and down on the waves of other people's events. Rather, we feel a compelling need to discover unfolding direction *from within. My* life. *My* reason for being. *My* unique story.

The storyteller's art has always been more than simply knowing how to communicate information. It is the gift of keeping a tale alive, ever moving, always unfolding with unexpected twists and turns that delight both the reader and the listener.

So too when men and women seek the meaning of their lives, they look for more than information about themselves. Beneath this search is a profound desire to experience an inner *unfolding* of their own personal stories. They want to experience *forward movement* that is uniquely their own. Not something programmed from outside, but an expression arising from deep within themselves.

An underlying instinct for a broader spiritual horizon animates this irrepressible longing. There is an opening *within the flow of ourselves*, an inner window through which the rising sun of a new creation can warm the next phase of evolution. It is sustained by fleeting glimpses into what human beings are in the process of becoming.

This is not some vision of where we can arrive and what we might achieve through personal effort. Rather, it is an unfolding, not of our making, that moves toward destinations beyond human comprehension. It has a different tempo and rhythm that beats beneath the ordered security we all program into our lives.

But we must come to know this transformation, learning the subtle signs that unfold this vast cosmic drama. There is a territory to be trodden within ourselves; it is to be observed, cultivated, and lived with through our personal seasons of joy, sorrow, expectation, passion, and gratification. We must each follow the thread of our own unique stories. We must wind along with them to find in the unfolding a rootedness in something greater than ourselves.

But where can we look within everyday experience for an entryway into such a surprise?

In our quest for an answer, let's look once again at those hurts and the blockage that for many people so rarely unfolds. A critical item that caught Eugene Gendlin's attention as a therapist was not the *content* of personal problems, but the *body's knowing or carrying* of those problems.

That's an important distinction! It identifies a privileged doorway through which the bio-spiritual can eventually appear.

From a therapeutic point of view, *how* a person carries a difficulty is often far more important than the *content* that is carried. Gendlin and other psychologists have noted that successful therapy involves more than a client's simply learning something new about himself or herself. Rather, success emerges from a distinct *physical shift* in the bodily sense of a problem or a life situation, a *felt shift* to use Gendlin's more technical phrase.

Dr. Gendlin observed with many people that although the content with which they worked might be painful, getting the correct symbol together with their felt sense always felt right and good. The problem was not necessarily solved, but the way that it was *carried* could be changed.

We received a touching illustration of this fact in a recent letter from one of our workshop participants.

Enclosed is the announcement of the birth of my son. Unfortunately, I was not able to have a natural childbirth as Jeremy went into fetal distress—so, I was put "under" and he was out within five minutes. So much for a drugless birth. He was a very sick baby—he had a blood transfusion in the first twenty-four hours, and oxygen for five days and finally he came home after twelve days in intensive care.

I am thankful that I attended the weekend of learning how to focus—as it helped me deal with what has happened.

Before I found out that he was a Down's Syndrome baby, I first was *very* upset at not experiencing any part of the birth—I felt so empty at having a life inside of me and then waking up with it gone—not even beside me. In fact, the situation of his birth is more difficult for me than having a handicapped child.

Using the focusing has helped me accept the situation of his birth and condition and not dwell on the "Why me?" question. I learned the important thing—that I love him, and God gave me a very special child.

In fact, I feel lucky because my life now has a specific direction—to help Jeremy develop to the best of his potential.

There are still many difficult moments, but with the help of prayer, focusing, relatives, friends and other Down's Syndrome parents it makes it a lot easier. Someday, I hope to return for a follow-up. Thank you again for teaching me.

Perhaps you know from personal experience what it means to be suddenly gifted with purpose and direction in your life. It may not always be what you would have chosen for yourself. Yet the unexpected arrival of such meaning can release enormous reserves of energy and, in some instances, lifelong commitment. Such an experience rarely provides a *solution* to the practical, sometimes tragic difficulties you may confront. But sitting down with a tragedy in a bodily way can sometimes bring a profound *resolution* in the way the pain is carried.

This is why the behavior of felt meaning is so different from the behavior of meanings that can be conceptualized and thought. The function of felt meaning is different. It's goal is different. The most important aspect of a felt sense is not content but movement. *It is meant to unfold!*

The initial obscurity of a felt sense, your feeling something without being able to label it accurately, lies not in some as yet unnamed and murky content. It is an incompleteness that arises from the *pre-process* nature of this experience. A felt sense is much like electrical power in a wire before the switch is thrown. It is meant to go somewhere, to move, to unfold. *Felt shift,* as we mentioned earlier, is the first forward movement of an implicit meaning.

Most people who seek change in their lives look upon their feelings as either good or bad. They feel good when they are happy and challenged. They feel bad if they are depressed and anxious. Personal change is usually thought of as some sort of transformation in the *content* that is felt. But such a view is not really on target. It doesn't pinpoint the actual source of frustration.

The central issue in any blockage to human growth has relatively little to do with the content of feeling and felt meaning. But it has everything to do with whether there has been *a breakdown of movement* in the unfolding of bodily felt meaning—the *felt shift* that Gendlin has identified.

It is an oversimplification to think of personal change as some sort of magical substitution that replaces bad feelings with good ones. If looked at superficially, this may appear to be what happens whenever things get better. But close examination will show that the *restoration of inner process* is the actual vehicle of transformation.

Happiness and enhanced social awareness come about not because we have *good* feelings rather than bad ones. It is because the very basis for healthy social functioning is restored. This happens whenever bodily felt meaning that has been blocked can move forward once again. Then we become more fully functioning and more social human beings.

Felt meaning, then, is always more than the particular content that may appear to give it substance at any given moment. Like a story, *it is meant to move forward*, to lead beyond itself. A vital aspect of this meaning, then, is its potential to act as an open-ended invitation drawing each person along a path of further unfolding.

Perhaps an example can illustrate our point. The two of us enjoy going on long mountain walks in the High Sierra, and we especially appreciate pausing by the small streams that carry runoff from melting snow packs. There is something about the rush of sparkling water over smooth boulders that works a special magic on one's capacity for presence. We usually just want to sit down and be quiet for a while, not thinking about anything in particular, but simply resting in the sound and its effect upon us. Eventually, however, we reach a degree of satisfaction, and our attention is invariably drawn upstream or downstream, and we begin hiking again along the water's edge. It is this ordinary experience of walking along an unfamiliar mountain stream that might help clarify what we now recognize as an important bio-spiritual dimension to bodily knowing.

As we walk, we take time for looking. We like to stop occasionally, pick something up, view a beautiful rock formation from different angles, or enjoy the physical sensation of jumping from one dry rock to another in the midst of rushing water. Our attention is momentarily directed toward many different sights, sounds, and sensations during our hike. All this describes the immediate *content* of our experience.

But there is another, possibly an even more important dimension to this awareness. It is the overriding *attraction* of the watercourse itself, which calls us to continue our journey up- or downstream. This attraction and the effect it has on us is like an everpresent melody or theme continually playing behind the individual stops we make to look, listen, and admire. The stream beckons us onward because there is always a new unfolding around the next bend.

This has led us to realize that a large part of the attraction we find hiking along the water's edge is not only the individual sights we see *but the actual unfolding itself.* How often we've glanced at our watches and finding it time to turn back have felt a mingled sense of frustration, annoyance, sadness and, perhaps most of all, a kind of longing as we looked toward the next bend around which we might never travel. Reason told us that behind the disappearing curve there probably lay more of the same water, tree stumps, bushes, and wildlife. Yet somehow this logical assurance never fully satisfied us. Walking the stream has come to symbolize for us the process of life and the process we feel every person is called to experience. *Felt meaning lies not only in what is found but in the process of unfolding itself!*

The very special attraction of hiking along a stream's edge includes not only the individual sights and sounds one stops to enjoy, but a beckoning mystery as well. It is the lure that continues to invite the traveler forward. Whenever one focuses one's attention upon a particular object, *it is always done within a broader context of movement, flow, journey, process, and continuing invitation.* While our immediate attention may be directed toward an individual scene that momentarily captivates us, we never really lose our sense for the hike and for the unfolding stream that is life.

Our point, then, is that there seems to be some *body of invitation* akin to this stream experience deep within each one of us. It appears as meaning that is felt, a meaning that flows and invites us, much like our journey along the water's edge.

Within this very movement a broader sense of "I" can appear.

What we are writing about in this chapter is our experience that Focusing awakens a felt sense of *process*. It unearths a knowing beyond the restrictions of *content*. Consciousness is always more than *what* we think. It is, simultaneously, a window on some wider identity. But the opening appears within the leading edge of our own personal story. Focusing helps us become aware of the movement, the *felt shift*, the *being carried forward*. It is within such an experience that we can be drawn *inside* the Mystery. This is an important realization about bio-spirituality that we have come to value over the years.

Someone once said that time, in addition to measuring motion, also has *density*. The center of a person's awareness *thickens*, so to speak, as more than separated individuality becomes involved. A person can have an awakening realization of *being within, being tied into, or being at home within* some Larger Process.

Obviously, this is a developmental experience, a *gradual* deepening of the sense a person may have for such somatic connectedness. We always recall with fondness a personal example used by Abraham Maslow to illustrate a time when he was drawn beyond the separated world of ego. It was a story he told about himself and his family. During the wintertime the Maslows would occasionally buy strawberries as a special treat. The whole family enjoyed them. After sitting down to eat, his two little girls would gobble up their berries while Maslow and his wife dawdled over theirs. It was, as he said, a game, because he and his wife knew what would happen next. As soon as the children had finished their own berries, they looked to their parents for more. Then, Maslow said, he and his wife would feed their own strawberries one by one to their daughters and, as he put it so well: "It may sound strange, but I enjoyed the taste of the strawberries more in my child's mouth than I did in my own." The line of separation had disappeared. The dichotomy had been transcended, if you want to say it in a technical way.

What we have here is a delightful tale of expanding human experience as it travels the road toward cosmic congruence. It is an embodied sense of being carried beyond stifling individuality and separateness.

Traditional psychology naturally fits the developing person within a chronological framework —birth, infancy, childhood, adolescense, adulthood, old age, death. The Greeks called this experience of time *chronos*. The term describes a continuum of past, present, and future. The experience of temporal succession is measured by clocks, the movement of planets, and the regular succession of day and night.

From a subjective point of view, *chronos* refers to an experience of time in which we relate principally to the outside surfaces of things. It speaks of calculating and manipulating situations in which control is a critical ingredient. *Chronos* measures the time needed to confront and solve problems, a time in which to get things done.

But what we are trying to describe here is an aspect of the evolving sense of "I." While *chronos* is experienced in the normal biological lifespan of each human organism, there is a still deeper movement and subjective experience that promises to transcend this more limited temporal framework.

That is perhaps why another Greek word for time found its way into New Testament usage. This term, *kairos*, refers to a bodily-felt sense for *the time within which personal life moves forward. Kairos* does not describe a temporal succession but rather an inner felt motion that is associated with awakening or realization. It is an unfolding within the very center of self-awareness.

Kairos, then, does not refer to the phenomenon of being spread out laterally in time, for surviving. It refers, rather, to a process of deepening within the present moment, being drawn *inside* the movement of one's own story. It is a time not for solutions but for resolution. When it is used in the Greek New Testament, *kairos* is linked with an experience of salvation. It is liberation from an excessively narrow and confining perception.

Focusing can never produce a *kairos* experience on demand. That, of course, is gift. But Focusing does dispose us, position us as it reaches toward this same realm of experiencing. It seeks a core within the person that transcends all our daily reactions.

Another kind of consciousness evolution matures within *kairos,* right inside the growth and decline of each physical organism. This extended perception and motivation seems to aim at something beyond physical integrity and survival. Personal unfolding and change take place within a framework of *chronos,* history, the growth and senescence of each physical organism. In a word, *the flesh.* Within this context life goes forward, the center of awareness develops, and identity undergoes continual transformation. Yet simultaneously an even more profound bio-spiritual birth can take place inside that felt movement where *chronos,* in a sense, stands still. This is the awesome threshold of a new sense of "I."

Beyond all our daily reacting lies a self that knows the way home! Focusing can help to unveil this transforming perception. The place of *connection* lies right within the *telling* of our own stories. These two go hand in hand. We find God or the Mystery of Human Destiny within the *surprise* around each new bend of our own unfolding. As Alan Watts once wrote when commenting on religious renewal, "We do not need a new religion or a new bible. We need a new experience—a new feeling of what it is to be 'I'."[1]

George Bernard Shaw once said that by the end of the twentieth century creative evolution would become a religion. There are clues within the

Christian tradition that also hint at just such an evolving fullness within the Self-Process. There is an amazing reminder of it in the New Testament that is repeated over and over again. The Christ always appears in the fullness of *kairos!* There is a *thickening* in time and the sense of self that reaches consummation, according to the Apostle Paul, at the moment of realization in *kairos* when God will be all in all.

While writing his Epistle to the Galatians, Saint Paul recorded his own halting steps into just such an unusual experience. In a rather remarkable utterance he exclaimed: "It is no longer I who live, but Christ who lives in me." *(Gal. 2:20 RSV)* Putting aside, for now, the framework of specifically Christian belief, and considering this statement for what it appears to be—an effort to describe a deeply moving human experience—we may have a good example here of what Alan Watts was trying to describe with his call for a new sense of "I." Paul became aware that his own identity as a person was integral to the expression of a much Larger Reality. He, the separate individual, Paul, was somehow "in Christ."

The Christ, for Paul, stood as a symbol for an even greater Body of Awareness within which individual consciousness gradually unfolds. Paul's inner experience may have signaled a dawning realization for him that each apparently autonomous person, each discrete, individual particle of organic flesh also participates as an integral part of the unfolding story of a much

Larger Whole. In a manner he did not fully comprehend, the Apostle found himself somehow drawn forward as a living cell within the process of this far greater organism. He experienced an advancing fullness within his own being, a development in Self-Awareness beyond anything that he as an individual was capable of.

The transformation in awareness apparently came for Paul when he realized that consciousness was not limited to people's experience of their own separated fleshly selves. In a way he could only dimly comprehend, the canvas upon which he now found his identity projected was far larger than he could ever have imagined. As Paul's consciousness was drawn beyond the limited world of rational content and control into the art of allowing, his awareness gradually unfolded to include and to express some greater Self-Process.

Paul quite literally began to have a new experience of "I," discovering the focal point of his awareness and identity in something far more profound than his ordinary sense of self. Paul, from the town of Tarsus, was literally carried light years beyond the center of experiencing with which he was most familiar.

Within the framework of Christian thought the sense of self emerging within each individual appears as the tiniest visible tip of human self-realization. The process is the message, and the message is the process. Unless we consciously enter into the process that we are, we don't get the message. There remains a depth, entered precisely through the movement of unique, personal unfolding, that reveals that the limited identity that each of us experiences in daily life is grounded in a still Larger Process, the ultimate source of consciousness aware of itself.

There is a rare term of obscure meaning in the New Testament, *pleroma*. The word signifies ripening *fullness*. A maturing within moments of *kairos*. There is a developmental note here. For Christians, the process that God has become within human history *is not yet fully achieved*.

Look, then, to the advancing edge of your own unique story for a window on bio-spiritual awareness. Here is where Focusing can help. It nourishes an inner bodily felt sense of movement—resolution! Letting go and allowing, which we wrote about earlier, encourage this seed of evolution within each one of us. They become part of the overall climate that can carry us forward into the next phase of consciousness. But it is the actual unfolding itself, an inner sense of one's own personhood *as process* that is the vehicle of bio-spiritual transformation. The mainstream of evolution operates along a broad front, and that front passes through every human being on the face of this globe.

"Behold, now is the acceptable time *(kairos)*." *(2 Cor. 6:2 RSV)* When the Rosetta Stone of embodied knowing is brought to bear upon the hidden message of Christian revelation, attention is directed not toward some stale content of knowledge but at the very process of felt becoming, the on-going story that each of us is at in the present moment. Within the heart of this movement lies a Greater Word waiting to become Flesh and to dwell among us.

6

An ancient perspective

The evolving body of spirit

Did you know that a honey bee colony functions as an *individual living organism?* All those thousands of darting forms are, in fact, a unified, integrated expression of one single, vibrating life! It's difficult to grasp this because our perception is attuned to *particularity*. We sense organisms, not The Organism. Our ability to perceive broader unities is, as yet, still undeveloped. But there are tantalizing clues. Dr. Eugene Gendlin writes:

> Your physically-felt body is in fact part of a gigantic system of here and other places, now and other times, you and other people—in fact, the whole universe. This sense of being bodily alive in a vast system is the body as it is felt from inside.[1]

What Gendlin touches on here is nothing new. Mystics have been saying the same sort of thing for centuries. But is there a bio-spiritual clue in this statement? A direction to follow? A path to explore?

Can one find here some hidden thread in the fabric of human unfolding? A slightly unravelled edge in the whole cloth? An opening through which to glimpse something of our own next step as a species on the planet earth?

It's time, now, for us to consider a few hiero-glyphs in the Judeo-Christian tradition. We can expand Gendlin's statement by entering the Semitic worldview. The purpose of this chapter is to share some information about an unusual per-spective. We'll begin by looking through other people's eyes, trying to understand how they viewed the world and themselves.

There are certain refinements within the Greek New Testament, precisions that shed light upon the perennial quest for an experience of deeper unity. We shall find these precisions useful as we broaden our appreciation of what Focusing is all about.

It is interesting, at the outset, to notice the remarkable fluidity and ease with which Old and New Testament authors slip back and forth between their descriptions of an entire tribe and the individual members of it. They seem to con-sider each individual and the overall group as somehow one. Scripture scholars familiar with this casual juxtaposition of the individual and the larger whole speak of *corporate personality*.

Soma, a Greek term used to describe what we generally mean by *body*, has overtones of this larger incorporation. The *soma* of each person and the tribal *soma* are not only inseparable but somehow coextensive. Corporate personality exhibits much the same organicity that we have noted in the bee colony. From a Semitic perspective, the individual member of a tribe actually stands for and sums up the particular group from which he or she has sprung. *All of the whole is in the part.* You never speak of one without including the other. There is here no sense of collectivity or aggregation, no parts outside of parts, just an appreciation of some primordial organicity or *bodily felt tied-togetherness.*

Focusing, we feel, opens a doorway to this remarkable perspective. It turns a person's awareness to a point of resonance within the body where a "felt sense" for such unity resides. This is not a thinking kind of thing. It is knowing in a different way. Focusing allows our consciousness to settle into that area in ourselves where there is physical *in-binding* with the rest of the cosmos. We may, at the time, be working on some personal problem. But we are dealing with it in a *somatic* rather than in a purely logical or rational way. We are "bodying" *in* it rather than thinking *about* it. Our attention may be directed toward the felt carrying of a particular issue, but in the process we have become immersed in *soma*. We are immersed in a bodily felt tied-in-ness without necessarily noticing it.

There is another interesting feature of *soma*. New Testament literature reveals a further piece of evolutionary information about this unusual perspective. Let's return once more to the honey bee colony as a way of approaching this additional revelation.

It is sad, but nonetheless true that bees no longer evolve along the *mainstream* of consciousness evolution. They are not called beyond their participation in the highly specialized colony body or *soma* that has enabled them to survive. There is no horizon to be crossed in their awareness. No beckoning adventure in consciousness. No bio-spiritual frontier. Instead, the colony is self-contained. Barring some catastrophic intervention, it is able to survive but it is no longer able to evolve.

This *self-contained* quality of *soma* is described in New Testament literature by another Greek word, *sarx*—which is literally translated as *flesh*.

Notice that *flesh* does not mean exactly the same thing as *body*. *Sarx* and *soma* are definitely related, but their New Testament use highlights a remarkable difference that goes to the heart of what bio-spirituality and Focusing are all about.

To appreciate the meaning of *sarx,* we must first note something of a primordial option faced by every subhuman species that has ever been touched by the forward thrust of evolution. In every case, the process of natural selection forced a kind of choice upon them. The option either to remain open, finding security by expanding their consciousness potential, or to close off with an efficient *specialization,* an effective *control* system that could maximize individual and species survival but only at the cost of sacrificing more open-ended awareness.

Teilhard de Chardin chronicled these events in his work as a paleontologist. The now extinct saber-toothed tiger's efficient adaptation for survival during its reign on earth also meant that it would never become the ancestor of mature human awareness. The very specialization itself, those magnificent canines and tearing claws, guaranteed a falling off from the mainstream of developing consciousness. This marvelous animal quite literally became its specialization. Awareness was frozen and conditioned by the very tools for survival, the specialization that developed through time in the *body* of this species.

Perhaps that's why it became extinct. The saber-toothed tiger could no longer adapt to a changing environment. There was not enough time in which to grow and develop a new set of tools, so the species eventually died out.

An ancient law of survival dictates that one does not casually barter hard-won gains on the playing field of life. There is strength and endurance in this. Continuity and direction emerge when the basics of survival are assured.

But there are perils as well. *Success often limits flexibility!* Attitudes and approaches harden. In a world where *development* is the norm, effective specialization frequently narrows the possibility for consciousness evolution. Survival, it seems, can be purchased at the expense of expanding awareness.

The primary axis of evolution must then turn elsewhere for a point of further breakthrough, seeking yet another interface where an openness for further advance can be found. Like water flowing downhill, evolution searches out the path of least resistance, *flowing wherever consciousness is, less conditioned by the specializations with which it survives!*

It is clear that the option to accept or reject this forward advance of consciousness is now, for us humans, *a choice.* Our organismic specializations for survival are no longer exclusively physical but psychological. Human beings are efficient tool-makers. We do not grow antlers or cloven hooves, specialized canines or claws. Our tools are not physically *built-in* to our bodies. The hand with its opposable thumb means that we can make a diversity of instruments that are separate from ourselves. We are freed from this kind of elementary choice or natural selection.

A human being's primordial options now lie more within the heart. The blessing here is that they are *more flexible.* These choices are not irrevocable. Once the antler has grown, once the claws are in place, *there is no turning back* for that species. For us, however, there is space for maneuvering. Our psychological specializations are more malleable. But the eventual choice still has overtones of our evolutionary origins. We are doing basically the same thing. We must opt for continued openness and advance or isolating closure, control, and specialization.

Carried to an extreme, voluntary closure in the human being marks the appearance of what biblical tradition speaks of as *sin*. When sin is looked at from a broader evolutionary perspective rather than from a narrow moral point of view, it means slipping away from the mainstream of advancing consciousness and deserting the bio-spiritual quest. It is a tragic option within the forward flow of ourselves, and there is profound social as well as personal heartbreak in such calamitous decisions. By refusing to be our own unfolding stories, we thereby diminish not only our isolated selves but also the unified thrusting of consciousness within all of humankind.

That is why the Bible poses another dramatic option to sustain the forward thrust of human evolution. It speaks of *metanoia*, conversion. A return to the way. It is a coming home once again in openness to the unfolding inner destiny that calls us ahead. It is a radical choice for the risks of development rather than secure specialization and control as the more profound response to being human.

Focusing occurs along this cutting edge of conversion and evolution within every person. There is a letting go and dropping of the reins, *allowing* some power beyond all our secure specializations to lead us ahead. Focusing takes place in the flesh (*sarx*) because it deals with a "felt" sense. But at the same time it looks beyond the flesh. Beyond self-containment. It reveals another potential, another capability that transcends all our striving

for control. Beyond individual *survival* lies a further possibility: the transforming call to *evolve!*

Sarx, then, is the body of fleshly specialization.
It is *soma* (whether individual, or extended like the
bee colony) that is geared for survival, but it is not
necessarily open to the further call of consciousness evolution. *Sarx* is self-containment, the
healthy drive toward self-determination, mainte-
nance of biological integrity, and psychological
automony.

We stress the word *healthy* because specialization
and control are, obviously, necessary for biological
survival. But human life is more than simply surviving. There is development and evolution as
well. *Sarx* is only one element in an overall pattern
of advancing consciousness. It is a vital ingredient,
but it is only a part of the picture.

This experience of consciousness is necessarily
mortal. Individuals die. Species fade away. The
soma of *sarx* is a fleshly body of death and decay. It
is the vehicle of consciousness *for a time*. It is frag-
ile and limited.

But the New Testament describes something
more. It reveals dramatic new perspective on the
process of human evolution. It tells of an awareness of greater connectedness and organicity that
appears within the *unfinished* character of human
existence. It is toward this unfinished edge that
Focusing directs our attention.

St. Paul and St. John describe the gradual
unfolding of *a new soma,* an advancing Body of
awareness that appears within the maturing of

consciousness itself. Here, at last, one awakens to the realm of bio-spirituality.

Not only is there species-wide kinship in the flesh *(sarx)*, a common rootedness in some greater *soma* of human mortality. There is also an incredible bond *in our very openness to evolution!* The human species is *somatic* in its self-containment *as well as* in its potential for further advance.

The New Testament seeks to describe a further dimension to *soma* that is of unimaginable magnitude and depth. It points to a radically transformed basis for human identity that carries us light years beyond our most cherished ties with the earth.

Just as *somatic* organicity bonds us to our fleshly origins in the drama of earth's rise to reflex awareness, so too, there appears to be an organicity in the forward flow of consciousness itself. The dawn of *a new soma* with roots and drawing power in something beyond self-contained survival.

The New Testament has a word to describe this emerging *soma* as it appears on the leading edge of the many stories which we are. It is *Pneuma*— Spirit, a *soma* of expanding human awareness. This remarkable word has been used throughout Christian literature to describe *the on-goingness, the open-endedness* of each person's individual story. It is the species-wide movement toward greater tied-in-ness. A *gift* that draws consciousness forward.

My life, *my* reason for existing, *my* unique story is always more than the repetition of a dead-ended specialization. My story is no tired tale of past survival and success. It is my ongoing journey into the

greater fleshly body of *sarx* as well as into the exciting edge of gift that leads me still further ahead.
There is a mysticism of nature that bonds all things
in the common heritage of earth and stars—and
yet, there is something more.

A Spirit of the Earth! An eruption within *sarx*.
The bursting forth of a seed resisting all entropy
and decay. We are all *sarx*—together with the earth
from which we spring. But we are *pneuma* as well.
We are drawn forward by that gifted power working through aeons of evolution that has brought
us to this point in ourselves—and now leads still
further beyond.

Christian tradition refers to this process as *a resurrection of the flesh*, the transcending of limited,
self-contained survival. It is being drawn beyond
the narrow world of control.

Focusing addresses this miracle as an integral
part of daily living. Resurrection is *now!* It is
developmentally present as the grain of mustard
seed. The Kingdom of Heaven is within. Focusing
can help find the vague, dim outline of this incredible Body of Spirit, a power beyond all *sarx*.

There have been serious misunderstandings
throughout Christian history about the true meaning of *flesh*. It has been loudly condemned by
some. A forlorn figure at the mercy of prim recti-
tude and narcissistic self-righteousness. Yet
despite these frenetic outbursts of self-rejection
where the overriding preoccupation of Christian
experience has all too often glorified a denial of
sarx, the drama of Incarnation has never been

completely obscured. Like a tender crocus in the springtime, it has endured the harsh winter of incredulity and religious abuse. The prologue to St. John's gospel can never be denied: "And the Word became Flesh *(sarx)* and dwelt among us." *(John, 1:14 RSV)* For the Christian, whatever there is of Mystery and transcendence in human life, it must necessarily be bound up with *sarx*. This basically open organism of ours, this heaving, sighing, singing mass of emotion and wonderment, courage and cowardice, passion, self-sacrifice and indifference is a crucible for the next forward step into who we ultimately are.

There is a profound vision of human possibility in the writings of St. Paul and St. John, a salvation history of cosmic proportion that sums up what we have briefly described of corporate personality, *soma*, *sarx*, and *pneuma*. All these elements come together into a challenging picture of *the possible human*.

The unified *soma* of humanity in *sarx* is the biblical *Adam!* For Christian believers, all of humankind is the body of Adam, the corporate personality of our fleshly origin. But because we can evolve, because the primary axis of consciousness evolution still courses through our human unfolding, we are opened in this gifted advance to perceive and to participate in the birth of a New Adam, a new corporate personality and *Soma* called *Christ*.

Teilhard de Chardin used the term *Christo-genesis* to describe the *developmental* character of this

Larger Body. He highlighted *the awakening* of a new *Soma*. "Body of Christ" names a transformation within the depth of human awareness itself.

A new Copernican revolution is now breaking upon the frontiers of consciousness. As humankind has been forced to relocate its place among the stars, it must now by the overwhelming demand of consciousness readjust its very perception of God. Dramatic in its consequences, we are entering a profound reorientation in perspective. It is a vital challenge for the Christian community. From the vantage point of human development, *the experience of Christian revelation is not first about God—but about ourselves!* Within an evolutionary framework, Trinity, Incarnation, Grace, Faith, Sacrament, and Christology—all are meant to describe an unfolding of human consciousness. They highlight aspects of *human self-awareness and human self-process.*

In this sense, then, a rediscovered Christian bio-spirituality could contain a message of incalculable value for the advancement of human evolution. There is information here. A vast, hidden message. But to experience this incredible resource, the Rosetta Stone of bodily awareness must be brought to bear upon precious clues in this ancient tradition. This leap into the body's knowing, however, has been tragically lost within most of Christianity today.

Yet perhaps the vision of Teilhard de Chardin and what might be described as the pragmatic mysticism of Eugene Gendlin can excite further exploration of this neglected realm within ourselves. Père Teilhard was well aware of the dynamic surge within consciousness as it responded to a call beyond the limited *soma* of nature's self-contained survival. Gendlin has reaffirmed that steps in the direction of this Larger Mystery are steps always taken within the richness of *sarx*. The Flesh! Our inner window on *pneuma* (spirit) is set in the world of *sensory awareness*, that marvelous tapestry of *meaning that can be felt*. It is here that the gift that draws us ahead is known as an incarnation, an enfleshment, an eventual resurrection.

Focusing looks toward just such *somatic* knowing. More than simply getting in touch with one's feelings, it seeks a unique edge in awareness where fresh new possibilities can emerge. Focusing identifies an opening within the fabric of human unfolding. It marks a way through to the Body of Spirit!

7

The body's approach to death

A story being born in every dying

Imagine what it would be like to be a tiny, unobtrusive observer within the womb when a new life was being formed. Over a period of nine months you could see the gradual growth of cells, muscle, bone, and tissue. The formation of tiny arms, legs, hands, and the emergence of facial features would be a marvel to behold. As growth progressed and life's miracle developed, a time would come when the spontaneous movement of a hand or foot would occur and you could be thrilled by what was taking place before you.

Then, at the appointed hour, there would be a terrific straining of muscles, the breaking of membranes, a gushing of fluids, and suddenly *life would be gone!* The womb would be empty, leaving only tattered remnants of a throbbing aliveness that you had been privileged to observe during the long period of gestation. From your restricted point of view, you would have to conclude that the life had gone out. It was no more. *It had died.*

Being confined within the womb would severely limit your perspective. Unless you began to sense that the bodily formation taking place before you was somehow organized for life *outside* the womb, the cataclysmic departure could only be viewed as an end to everything. The quintessence of death itself.

However, a very perceptive observer might get some inkling of the larger life-process that the fetus was destined for by examining the limbs and sense organs as they matured in preparation for life *outside* the womb. These feet were made for walking! These eyes were made for seeing! This nose was made for breathing—but not in the warm, dark, watery womb.

Tiny feet, hands, nose, eyes, and ears all tell the perceptive observer something about what is yet to come. They represent *traces* within a limited uterine perspective of what lies beyond the next horizon. They are harbingers of the sensory world ahead.

This womb image came to us during a period of concentrated Focusing in preparation for the funeral of a dear friend. While we were sitting quietly with all the memories and felt knowing that stirred within us, we waited until this thought-provoking symbol brought about a shift in our bodily awareness, a felt transition in how the event could be carried.

The fear of death can be resolved in our bodies, not solved with our minds. There is no *answer* to the dreadful specter of total annihilation. No *solution* that soothes the mind's shattered logic. But there is response within the body. A felt naturalness, perhaps even rightness, about the experience, as though some inward organismic knowing recognizes death as a vital transition. Something is born in every dying! A believing is born of change.

Focusing can begin to transform one's perception, not through an *explanation* of death, but by providing a different place to stand within ourselves. This shift in perspective may itself be the answer that so many people seek.

Focusing draws our awareness toward the inner world of bodily meaning and felt movement. We approach death through a different kind of knowing. There is no bright flame of rationality here with which to pierce the gloom of dying. Just a *felt conviction* that grows to become far more satisfying than all the feverish explanations that reason can provide.

When Teilhard de Chardin reflected on the probable coming of an "ultra-humanity," he challenged us to look beyond the narrow perceptual framework with which we are so familiar. His conclusion as a paleontologist was that

> Our present condition is still so immature that Mankind in its existing form . . . cannot be scientifically regarded as anything more than an organism which has not yet emerged from the embryonic stage.[1]

Perhaps even now we feel this womb-like condition. All around us the periphery of consciousness fades off into dark unknowing. Reason can never penetrate this inky void. But our bodies, in their own way, may see farther than we realize.

There is an initial awareness in the feet, hands, and eyes of every fetus before birth. Some dim perception of purpose and finality. Perhaps a yearning to exercise the functions for which they have been fashioned.

Can our bodies even now hint at such subtle knowing? Is there a *language* deep within present experience that yields a trace of wider awareness? Are we on the road toward yet another birth? The light of a new day dawning?

Occasionally, in our reading of certain creative authors we have been touched by passages that speak of a wider scope of human consciousness. Suddenly a passage leaps out with a bodily-felt drawing power and energy far beyond the matter-of-fact information it may contain. For example, William James, in a cautious statement that concludes his monumental work on *The Varieties of Religious Experience,* summarized his findings about such an experience as follows:

> Disregarding the over-beliefs, and confining ourselves to what is common and generic, we have in *the fact that the conscious person is continuous with a wider self through which saving experiences come,* a positive content of religious experience which, it seems to me, *is literally and objectively true as far as it goes.*[2]

While reading this passage for the first time, we were struck by James's notion of continuity with some "wider self." Our response was immediate and tangibly organic. Something felt right about the statement as, in much the same fashion, it might feel right for a fetus to flex its muscles and kick in the womb without really knowing what such kicking was about.

This is not a rightness that is easily analyzed with logic and reason. It cannot be reduced to categories of cause and effect. Yet something in the body feels at home with such a statement. At least it did for us.

On another occasion several years ago we had been reading Dom Sebastian Moore's challenging book, *God Is a New Language*. A passage stood out at that time and is still vivid to us:

The human body is not a sort of super-expensive toy. It is very misleading to call it *your* body: to exist in the body means to be bound by a thousand ties into the whole bundle of existence. This in-binding, which is beyond our personal control, is us just as much as what we call "I" is us.[3]

Again, the same felt wonder, and the feeling of being on target. The body said "Yes!" in a way quite unlike what the mind might say. The felt meaning of this passage, for us, was far different from any *thinking* of it. There was deeper resonance. Some untapped reserve of knowing was called into play.

On another occasion we were reading from Karl Rahner's article "Christology and an Evolutionary World View." Again, the same felt sense emerged.

Matter is presently at a stage where, in man, it is conscious of itself and of its relation to reality as a whole and to the source of its existence. . . . The material world is to some extent the one body of a manifold self-consciousness incorporating that body into the relation to its infinite source. And if cosmic consciousness has reached its first step in man, it must continue to develop. Through his body man is allied to the whole cosmos and communicates with it. In their role as reference point of the spirit, body and cosmos together press on to ever greater consciousness.[4]

Our response to this somewhat academic philosophical reflection was later felt with even greater intensity when we were reading a brief passage from the theoretical physicist, Sir Arthur Eddington. His novel view of ultimate reality once again sparked in us a deeper felt meaning. The written conclusion found a receptive audience within the body's sense for direction and purpose in the cosmos.

To put the conclusion crudely, the stuff of the world is mind stuff . . . Consciousness is not

sharply defined, but fades into sub-con-
sciousness and beyond that we must postu-
late something indefinite but yet continuous
with our mental nature . . . It is difficult for
the matter of fact physicist to accept the view
that the substratum of everything is of mental
character . . .

Not in the dim past but continuously by
conscious mind is the miracle of creation
wrought. The idea of a universal Mind or
Logos would be, I think, a fairly plausible
inference from the present state of scientific
theory; at least it is in harmony with it . . .
Religion first became possible for a reason-
able scientific man about the year 1927.[5]

We recall a film about severely disturbed children who were being cared for in a family-style setting, seven or eight youngsters living in a house
with two adult counselors. In one memorable scene
a nine-year-old boy climbed to the top of a tall cab-
inet and refused to come down. He was yelling
obscenities at everyone within earshot like a little
rooster crowing from the rooftop. The counselors
cajoled, bantered with him, and even taunted him.
Gradually, the edge of humor began to creep in.
The small, fiercely determined youngster would
yell, scream, and then turn away to giggle. An
obscenity would end on a half-repressed laugh.
The counselors knew what was happening and
kept the process going. Finally the boy allowed
himself to be pulled down to a loving hug with one

more layer removed from his protective armor. A small step was taken away from the darkness of egoism. A brief flash of salvation, like a welcome meteor brightened the dark night of a tiny, tortured life. Faith, at last, had arrived. The believing born of change. With humor and love came a friendlier place inside. The inner landscape was different.

Each of the passages we have just cited called forth a similar friendly space—a point of cosmic connectedness within bodily knowing. The specter of death is resolved in the body, not solved with the mind. That is the leap of faith. We wonder, now, whether such gifted moments represent a trace of broader awareness, some felt sense for "a wider self through which saving experiences come."

There is an interesting clue in the Bible about such an expanding experience. The hint comes from another special word in the Greek New Testament. St. Paul writes of such Larger Awareness as *Musterion*, The Mystery. *Musterion* is the greater Whole within which we fit as parts. Yet, at the same time, this greater Whole is expressed *in* us. All of the Whole is in every part.

Ordinarily, *Musterion* is translated into the Latin scriptures as *Mysterium,* "Mystery." But occasionally another word is used instead: *Sacramentum.* Our English word *sacrament* comes from this. It is sometimes translated in the New Testament as "secret" or "hidden purpose."

He has made known to us his hidden purpose [*Musterion/Sacramentum*]—such was his will and pleasure determined beforehand in Christ —to be put into effect when the time [*kairos*] was ripe [*Pleroma*]: namely, that the universe, all in heaven and on earth, might be brought into a unity in Christ. *(Eph. 1:9–10 NEB)*

Most Christians think of Sacrament as one of the seven sacraments like Baptism or Matrimony. But there is a broader psychological sense behind the meaning of this sign/action. Sacraments exist within the Christian community in order to foster an awareness of the innate sacramentality of human existence itself.

There is hidden purpose within the gift of life. There is a secret *interface* through which one can be drawn forward toward greater awareness. A sacramental attitude is essentially one of openness to this larger picture, an inner appreciation of the movement that draws us ahead. It involves a commitment to living in that movement. One may refer to this unfolding as Body of Spirit or the Self-Process, but what sacrament really implies is an alertness for signs of hidden purpose. There is an expectation that every act, every thought, no matter how ordinary, offers a potential doorway to our own and the world's evolution.

This reminds us of an image that Pete often uses. One day while he was seated at his desk, he was idly looking out the window after a rainstorm. Droplets of water dotted the pane in front of him. As the sun came out from behind a cloud, Pete watched the play of light and color in the drops. Suddenly he realized that each drop of water contained the same image reflected from outside the window. The corner of our house was clearly visible in every drop. Each contained an image of this larger whole. Each reflected that whole. Each was an avenue of access to something beyond itself. The sacramental side of human existence speaks of this underlying connection.

If there is promise of immortality and some potential for identity continuity that even now transcends the grim prospect of final extinction, it will most probably be found in whatever we can experience of sacramental unfolding within ourselves. Here at last we may find a potential "lookout point in the universe," some hint in our womb-like existence of greater life to come.

There is profound sacramentality at work in Focusing whenever the felt sense unfolds. A connection appears within that very movement that carries us forward. The "felt shift." Because there is a letting go, a kind of dying, new life can appear. Death is followed by resurrection.

But this Larger Picture unfolds within the living flesh (*sarx*) of each individual person, much as the image of our house appeared whole and intact within each raindrop. Individuality, therefore, is the stuff within which this greater awareness occurs. Uniqueness is important. It can never be abandoned.

Focusing, perhaps, can unveil this sacramental opening within our inner universe. There is a subtle trace of light that indicates that the darkness of our womb-like and all too often separated existence is only a prelude to an even greater awakening.

Death for us humans may be a kind of ultimate sacrament, a final step into the body's knowing that reveals some "hidden purpose," a friendly place on the far side of ego. There is a seed within *sarx*, a secret waiting to burst forth within the very consciousness that rebels against dying.

Is each of us an unfolding felt sense within some Greater Awareness? Does a Deeper Source, a Wider Self, a Universal Mind or Logos *focus upon* us as the personal edge of its own unique unfolding? Are we raindrops on some cosmic window, extending consciousness one step further into the darkness of matter itself?

Should death be feared any more than some timorous felt sense that might fear the rush of awareness carrying it forward toward greater Fullness *(Pleroma)*? What, after all, does our bodily felt meaning really have to fear? *It is already one with that which it is in the process of becoming!*

8

Toward a new paradigm for Western spirituality

Carl Jung once described a tragic irony he had observed in the lives of many Christians.

> That I feed the hungry, that I forgive an insult, that I love my enemy in the name of Christ— all these are undoubtedly great virtues. What I do unto the least of my brethren, that I do unto Christ. But what if I should discover that the least amongst them all, the poorest of all the beggars, the most impudent of all the offenders, the very enemy himself—that these are within me, and that I myself stand in need of the alms of my own kindness—that I myself am the enemy who must be loved— what then? As a rule, the Christian's attitude is then reversed; there is no longer any question of love or long-suffering; we say to the brother within us "Raca," and condemn and rage against ourselves. We hide it from the world; we refuse to admit ever having met this least among the lowly in ourselves. Had it been God himself who drew near to us in

this despicable form, we should have denied him a thousand times before a single cock had crowed.[1]

What a paradox! What an enigma that this disabling experience should be fed by the paralyzing impotence of Christian spirituality whenever it confronts the specter of self-hatred. Instead of responding with a healing *process*, what is provided is information. This sort of approach is misguided and ineffective. The articulation of ideals and values, the teaching of biblical narratives, explaining theological truths about God's love and the "saying of prayers" do not create the psychological climate and quality of self-presence within which human wholeness and a more loving person can emerge. Responding with religious ideas and ideals does not support that leap into body consciousness that spirituality, love, and human maturing are really all about. As a result, the love that so many sincere Christians want to share with others they can hardly extend to themselves.

Christian spirituality has yet to resolve this split between loving one's neighbor and loving one's self. Churches still do not understand that all the preaching and teaching of theological truths and ideals will not make this problem go away. The neglect of body consciousness is an enormous obstacle both to human maturing as well as to spiritual growth. Jung always hoped that some day Christianity would recognize the body's integral role in consciousness evolution and spiritual development.

If we can reconcile ourselves with the mysterious truth that spirit is the living body seen from within, and the body the outer manifestation of the living spirit—the two being really one—then we can understand why it is that the attempt to transcend the present level of consciousness must give its due to the body.[2]

Christian spirituality, however, still lacks an effective praxis that can bring these two together within experience. Whatever direction pastoral ministry and spirituality may travel in the future, they will certainly need to address the continuing tragedy of self-hatred in a far more effective fashion. Radical change will be necessary if a new paradigm for Western spirituality is to emerge from Christianity. Without drastic course correction, this ancient tradition will simply go on contributing to the problem rather than offering an effective solution.

Any theology that is compatible with the human growth process is still only information. As such, it remains powerless to effect transformation when pain, fear, and self-hatred are present and carried in our bodies. Every such attitude, after all, grows out of a *felt sense*. The fear and rejection that so many people feel toward themselves can only be healed by owning and listening to the bodily-felt sense out of which all this negativity arises.

Christian churches, of course, are not the only places where this bodily felt awareness is tragically ignored. A far broader cultural neglect extends this attitude into health care, education, politics, social programs, and penal institutions. But the churches may be in a unique position to bring about significant social change if they can first put their own houses in order. Any new paradigm for Western spirituality must actually take a leap into body consciousness rather than simply talking about it theologically.

This need to heal self-hatred highlights one of the critical issues facing Western spirituality. Our human survival depends upon the resolution of this catalyst for massive self-destruction. But there is yet another problem of enormous significance for growth and survival.

We turn once again to Carl Jung for a concise statement of the issue. It surfaced in a comment he made on the relationship between yoga and Christianity.

Jung clearly identifies a lopsided mind-set that any effective Western spirituality must counteract. We call attention to this limited perspective because it can also distort and frustrate the Focusing process.

> Western man has no need of more superiority over nature, whether outside or inside. He has both in almost devilish perfection. What he lacks is conscious recognition of his inferiority to the nature around and within him. He must learn that he may not do exactly as he wills . . . Since Western man can turn everything into a technique, it is true in principle

that everything that looks like a method is either dangerous or condemned to futility. Insofar as yoga is a form of hygiene, it is as useful to him as any other system. In the deepest sense, however, yoga does not mean this but, if I understand it correctly, a great deal more, namely the final release and detachment of consciousness from all bondage to object and subject . . . My criticism is directed solely against the application of yoga to the peoples of the West . . . Western civilization is scarcely a thousand years old and must first of all free itself from its barbarous one-sidedness. This means, above all, deeper insight into the nature of man. But no insight is gained by repressing and controlling the unconscious, and least of all by imitating methods which have grown up under totally different psychological conditions. In the course of the centuries the West will produce its own yoga, and it will be on the basis laid down by Christianity.[3]

Yoga, for Jung, is more than mere mental hygiene. It is, in his view, the disciplined commitment to that gift of consciousness and experience that lies beyond the realm of deliberate control. For this reason he regarded the Western tendency to acquire control through technique as a serious obstacle to human and spiritual maturity.

We raise this issue because the overwhelming need for power over nature can introduce a subtle temptation even into the Focusing process. It is a

temptation that grows stronger with each successful application to the crises and brush fires of
daily life. A person can gradually come to regard
his or her Focusing as nothing more than *technique*. A convenient tool. Something done in order
to feel better. Before long, Focusing can be
directed toward inner hurts much as one applies
medicine to a wound. Little by little it becomes
natural to try to turn this activity into *a new form of
control*. No step-by-step psychological process is
immune from this kind of misuse, even one whose
essential psychological dynamic is the letting go
of control. Focusing, too, can become just one
more instance of a Western approach to "the
nature around and within" us.

The catch, however, is that for Focusing to
work, a person must first *let go* of the need to be in
charge of each felt sense. And as soon as a person
finally does let go and experiences resolution in
bodily knowing, something deep inside usually
wants control over this very process so that it can
be repeated again and again at will. This is a
strange paradox, this creeping back into awareness of a desire for greater control by "letting go."

But the success of Focusing lies in treating it as
far more than a technique that we do on our own.
*Focusing becomes an effective agent of healing trans-
formation not because we do it, but because we, finally,
can allow it to do itself!*

This is not mere playing with words. Something radically different operates throughout the

Focusing process. "Letting go" and "allowing" unveil a new horizon within bodily knowing. People who live with this dimension of themselves every day gradually come to relish being surprised by what their bodies know about meaning and direction in life. In time, a dedication and commitment can develop toward making space for this transformed way of being.

As this happens, we find Focusing valued in a different way. While still prized as a helpful approach for dealing with difficult things, it is cherished even more as a doorway of bio-spiritual awareness. Out of this experience deeper questions of meaning can be addressed.

Focusing offers a practical alternative to those spiritual practices that fail to resolve the destruction and pain of self-hatred. It opens a doorway into the body that is rich in an experience of mystery, gift, and surprise. But the one who focuses must grow in the realization that bodily knowing is filled with more than what we achieve by the power of our own hands. Focusing directly counteracts the mind-set of which Jung wrote earlier, but not without the continuing disposition of "letting go."

Before bringing this book to a close, let us briefly share a final reflection on why we believe Focusing, together with certain ancient teachings in the Judeo-Christian tradition, can make a significant contribution to an evolving new paradigm for Western spirituality.

The "rediscovery" of the body in our age and culture has opened a critical threshold in spiritual awareness. A dialogue, hopefully, will soon begin between an ancient faith struggling to find its voice in this age of perpetual transition and the ring of a fresh new humanism that reaches for faithfulness to its own deepest yearnings. In union with one another they must find some way to go beyond the overriding need for control as well as that hardening core of fear, mistrust, and self-hatred that permeates so many lives today and threatens the specter of a nuclear nightmare.

One theologian, Gregory Baum, has tried to express the presence of God in a new language. It is a language that is as understandable to the modern humanist as it can be to a believer in an ancient tradition. He writes of prayer, a somewhat undervalued commodity in our modern, secular world. Undervalued, that is, until each of us senses within our own life struggle the neglected message of Western spirituality.

> To pray is to be in touch with oneself in a new way: to listen to the melody, not made by our- selves, that sounds at the core of our being and, from beyond the sickness that deafens us, summons us to be alive. Since God is redemptively present in man's coming to be, prayer is a way of holding or possessing one- self. This kind of prayer is not a moving away from oneself and reaching out for another, but rather a being in communion with oneself

across many obstacles, and a laying hold of oneself in and through the gift dimension that is constitutive of one's being.[4]

Baum describes the sheer organicity of grace at work in bodily knowing. The kingdom of heaven is within. It is a "gift dimension that is constitutive of one's being."

Abraham Maslow echoed much the same sentiment.

A whole school of psychologists now believe that "spiritual values" are *in* the organism, so much a part of the well-functioning organism as to be *sine qua non* "defining-characteristics" of it.[5]

What links Western science with the Judeo-Christian tradition is the common ground of bodily knowing. Here there is room for a mutual bio-spiritual perspective. A common "lookout point in the universe." Focusing helps awaken an organismic sense for some inner power and *gift* beyond anything that we could ever contrive. It is coming in touch "across many obstacles" with a melody that calls us to life. Focusing opens the possibility that a process of resolution may go forward *in our bodies*. From a Christian perspective, this is the stuff of *grace* and *incarnation*. This is not more information, but touching and being touched by the very realities that theology describes so abstractly.

Christianity has preserved a wisdom tradition about "the gift dimension of our being." It is not only information, but experience as well. Yet these riches have hardly been tapped. And there is still so much more: the appreciation of *Soma* and Spirit; a tied-in-ness to cosmos and beyond; a marvelous sense for movement, development, and an unfolding into the inner life of God. We are all, according to Christian revelation, the Body of Adam and—within some vast evolutionary unfolding—an emerging *Soma* of Christ. We are bound together by *chronos* and *sarx* (the flesh), yet touched by the fullness of time in *kairos*. The kingdom of heaven *is* within. But a way home to realizing all this still sleeps soundly inside bodily knowing. The Rosetta Stone of consciousness has only been barely unearthed.

If there is common ground between Maslow and Baum it lies in their mutual respect for the human body and some sense, however vague, for the "gift dimension of our being." Much within the Christian tradition still remains hidden from the perspective of bodily knowing. But the experience of *gift* and a commitment to *incarnating presence* within the felt sense of each passing moment—that is readily available. Now!

Grace and Incarnation. One can begin here the quest for a new paradigm, the search for a uniquely Western yoga. We are coming home, finally, to the Mystery of Body Consciousness/ God Consciousness.

Appendix 1

An updated summary of Focusing steps

(as we teach them)

> **Note:** *The authors, the Institute for Bio-Spiritual Research, and our publishers do not teach Focusing or promote Focusing Companions either as a substitute for professional psychotherapeutic or psychiatric care for those who need it, nor as a substitute for training and licensing in the above health care fields.*

Focusing is a very personal, caring, and gentle way of being with yourself or another. You might even use the word **reverent**. It is not **pushing** to get somewhere. Even though you may think you know what needs to happen in another person or yourself, the body's wisdom rarely follows a path laid down by the mind. You are doing something quite **different** when you focus; **allowing** a process to go forward. You're leaving yourself open to be drawn in a direction you might never have previously considered.

During Focusing you want to find some way to be with negative feelings and issues that is different

from the usual holding them at arms length or trying to avoid them. Being "caring" with an issue
means that at least for this Focusing session you try
to remain open to all that is there without immediately seeking to control it, make it better, or make it
go away. Feelings change **as** they unfold, **as** they
are heard, **as** they tell their uniquely felt stories.

The Steps of Focusing are taught in many different ways and with quite diverse emphases. In
the following pages we summarize the Focusing
Steps as well as the way in which we teach
Focusing throughout our bio-spiritual network.
We also share some of the reasons why we have
settled on our approach over others. The outline
we follow covers four main areas:

- Why we teach Focusing the way we do
- Short Form Focusing
- Long Form Focusing steps with an Inventory
- Further suggestions for guiding

Why we teach Focusing the way we do

Many teachers of Focusing begin with the skill of
Rogerian active listening as a preparation for
learning to focus and guiding others. We tried that
for a number of years, but then switched to staying
with and emphasizing the Focusing process itself.

When saying this, we in no way denigrate the value of active or "healing" listening. But we found that emphasizing the listening skill at the same time we were teaching Focusing tended to confuse people. Active listening takes an enormous amount of time and energy to do well and, in itself, is an art form. The problem we found was that while the person listened to often feels heard, he or she does not necessarily experience the inner change that can come from Focusing.

When Ed trained with Carl Rogers he found that he often spent an enormous amount of time listening, but with very little significant **movement** taking place within the client. In listening, the structure is not fine-tuned enough to draw the person who is sharing right into the body-priority. Instead, the one sharing can go around in circles, skirting the periphery of what needs to be held in the body, while the one listening simply has to accompany them on this merry-go-round. From our experience, teaching people silently to be in their bodies, listening to the body-priority, has a much greater chance of being on target than we have experienced with verbalizations.

Active listening sessions easily become training sessions for therapists rather than sessions within which people experience forward movement within the process of Focusing. As Ed so often says, he got a sense for reflective listening from Rogers, but he did not experience an inside feel for movement within the client until he learned Focusing from Eugene Gendlin, the originator of

Focusing who was an early graduate student and colleague of Rogers.

Our question has always been, "How can we most effectively facilitate human wholeness?" Experience has shown that listening sessions very easily turn into **sharing** sessions rather than **process** sessions for untrained people because they have no inner sense for what the process of wholeness is all about. Focusing gets right to the point. Also, when listening is given first priority, Focusing begins to take second place as people concentrate on refining their listening skills.

There is another reason we begin with Focusing and don't emphasize listening skills until later. What people need in the beginning, even more than an ability to listen, is **some simple way to hold in their bodies and "own" negative feelings**. You can go on listening forever and neither the listener nor the one listened to have any idea what to do with or how to be with hurting places. Experience over the last twenty years has taught us what the priorities are. We plunge people directly into **"caring-feeling-presence,"** *(described in the "note" in Long Form Focusing Step 3)*—how to be with scary places—and you can't do that without Focusing.

To start with, Active Listening is the therapist's way of looking at things. It avoids the basic issue of both people journeying together in the pain of one of them, without any of the supports you can get by **talking**. People need to be invited to enter directly into their process—"What's between me and feeling really good right now?"

Secular priorities are quite different from those we emphasize in a bio-spiritual approach. Bio-spirituality highlights an experience of grace in the body, or "letting go and letting God" as this is often put in AA circles. Such a priority supercedes for us the learning of listening skills, valuable though these may be.

Behind all our priorities lies one that is most important for the use of psychological processes in spirituality. It is enabling people to let go into the truth of themselves, especially their brokenness, in order that they may bodily experience **grace** within the process of their growth into wholeness.

Moreover, it is through the experience of companioning or journeying together as the focuser takes the risk with the guide to be vulnerable and own that brokenness in his or her body that the **Focusing Companions** experience begins to surface. This is a stage of growing together where no longer is the relationship one of doctor to patient, therapist to client, teacher to pupil. Rather, it becomes one in which there is **empowerment in mutual vulnerability**. Ed says more about this in his booklet on **Focusing Companions**, *(which may be obtained by writing the Institute for Bio-Spiritual Research)*. Once again, though, we feel that this experience does not happen as effectively when people simply concentrate on the development of listening skills.

Let's turn, now, to our outline of the Focusing Steps. We can preface our remarks by summarizing five important learnings that guide us toward Focusing:

- My body knows things as well as my head.

- How does my body try to tell me what it knows? Through feelings, body-sensations, and things I know but can't yet put in words. We call these *felt senses*.

- Therefore, my body has its own language through which it wants to talk to me. There is always a story waiting to be told in my body whenever I notice feelings, sensations, and felt senses.

- How do I let my body tell its stories? By learning a special way of caring for, holding, and listening to my body's language.

- This special way of owning my body is called *Focusing*.

Short Form Focusing

The main difference between Short Form and Long Form Focusing in the following pages is that the Long Form contains instructions for an "Inventory," which is not included in the Short Form. The Inventory is useful when you find yourself overwhelmed with many issues, or when after growing quiet nothing seems to surface, or if there are several issues and you can't sense a clear priority. The Long Form also contains more in-depth explanations and suggestions. These pages will be your most useful resource for better understanding what is happening in each Focusing Step as well as what to say if you are a guide. The Short Form will get you more quickly into the actual body-feel of Focusing.

Use Short Form Focusing whenever you have a feeling that is clamoring for your attention—a spontaneously given Number One. Use it, also, when you want to check in and see how things are going without taking time to go through an Inventory and set issues aside, one by one.

After taking a moment to grow quiet inside, here are some questions that will help guide your Focusing:

a) Ask yourself, "What feels like it most needs listening to inside me right now?" Take time to notice what that is. Notice where you feel it and how it feels in your body.

b) Then ask yourself: "Is it OK to be with it right now?" If the answer is YES, continue with (c) and (d). If the answer is "NO," ask, "Can I be with my feeling of not wanting to be with this?" If that is still not acceptable, then ask: "What can I be with?"

c) If the issue is one that doesn't feel good, sense whether you can give it some caring-presence (cf. note on caring-feeling-presence in Long Form, Step 3). Notice how it feels to be with it this way. Then, ask yourself:

d) "Can I let myself feel the whole thing in an open, gentle way, waiting for something to come—a word, a feeling, an image, a memory—that fits the way it feels?" If the answer is "YES," go to (e), if "NO," Ask yourself: "Is it OK to be with the feeling of not wanting to get near it?"

e) If something comes, notice how this feels in your body (don't just try to figure it out with your head). If it's OK to continue, stay with the body-feel of whatever came, allowing your inner story to unfold until it feels right to stop.

f) If nothing comes, or you have to stop before finishing, always promise this unfinished place that you will come back to listen again. If it helps, ask whatever feels incomplete inside: "How do you need me to be with you until you are ready to tell me your story?"

g) If something has unfolded, take time to notice the difference in how it feels now as contrasted with how it felt when you started. Allow time to savor and especially note the body-feel of that change. Finally, you might want to linger in gratitude with the feel of this gifted movement before stopping.

Long Form Focusing steps with an Inventory

Note: The following pages are meant to be used as a reference resource for learning to focus and guiding others in Focusing. Once you have studied and worked with these pages a few times, we encourage you to make your own simplified one page version of the Long Form Steps, being guided by the careful wording and key phrases printed below. Your personalized single page will make it easier to follow the basic Focusing movement both for yourself and while guiding another. The more expanded version given below can then be used as a resource to fall back on when needed. The reflection and study necessary in order to compose your own more brief (but, nonetheless, complete) version of the Long Form Steps will greatly help you to remember the sequence of these steps.

In the text that follows, suggestions for what to say are in plain type, instructions and explanations are in italics.

Preparation

The aim of this preparation exercise is to help the focuser grow quiet inside. It is not for the purpose of relaxing or numbing feelings. If there is anxiousness or tension, the preparation exercise helps to quiet the mind's chatter so the one Focusing can attend more carefully to whatever feelings are present in the body. Do not encourage the focuser to "relax." This just triggers all their habitual numbing mechanisms for blotting out feeling. Use the preparation exercise especially when you sense a lot

*of thinking and chatter in the head. The rationale
behind the preparation exercise is that the simplest
way to get out of the mind is to get into the body.
When your attention is on body-feelings, you can't
be thinking at the same time. If the focuser is clearly
in touch with body-feeling, then dispense with the
preparation exercise and go directly to Step 1.*

Take a few moments and allow your attention to
settle down into your solar plexus area. Ask yourself, "How does it feel in here?" Notice any body
language that tells you how it is inside right now.
If you find something there, then just attend to it
quietly for a few moments, noticing as much of the
feel of it as you can . . . *(pause)* . . . If nothing special
comes to your attention, then let your awareness
move around inside your body until you come to
another place where you notice any feeling and
pause there, carefully noticing whatever it is like
inside. For example, you might find an uneasiness
in your breathing, stiffness in your neck, heaviness
in your legs—something like that, where attending
to some identifiable sensation or feeling for a few
quiet moments will help you to move out of head
thinking and into your body's language. *(Pause)*

1. *Finding a space by taking an Inventory*

The purpose of Step 1 is to allow an opportunity for the focuser to identify whatever issues lie between him or her and feeling really good or free right now. Often, we go in circles, overwhelmed by so much going on inside us that we really don't know where to begin. We remain stuck and paralyzed, trying to figure things out with our heads and getting nowhere. Step 1 gets the body involved in setting priorities. It helps to identify and set things down one at a time so we're not just a jumbled up mess inside. This first Step provides needed distancing so we're not so paralyzed by the whirlpool of emotion. On the far side of all the "stuff" between me and feeling really good, there lies a core OK-ness. It helps to touch this place, even though each of us still has to go back and work through all our unfinished issues. Otherwise, we remain chronically dis-eased and consider this normal.

A. Now, let me know if something comes when you ask yourself: "Is there anything in my life right now keeping me from feeling really good?" *(Pause) Notice the careful wording of this question. You, as guide, invite the focuser to ask him/herself if there is anything in "my" life right now keeping "me" from feeling really good? This is another way to emphasize that the one Focusing is the one who is in charge. The guide is not an authority figure to whom the focuser responds. This is an inner dialogue. The guide's role is simply to be a companion on this inner journey.*

If the focuser doesn't respond after some time, the facilitator might ask: "Did anything surface?" If the answer is "Yes" go to [B]; if the answer is "No," say: "Let me know if something comes when you ask yourself: 'is there anything in my life right now that feels important enough to be with in a Focusing way?'" *If something comes, then go to Step 3, "Is it OK to be with this?"*

B. All right, now see if you can put this whole thing temporarily aside by imagining yourself setting it on the floor beside you . . . (or on a shelf, or in a container like a box—whatever image helps you to take it out of yourself for the time being, giving you the feel of some space between you and this whole thing) . . . Let me know if you are able to do this or not. *(Pause)*

Setting issues down is a way of getting distance from them. This is not pretending that they no longer exist. The purpose of the Inventory is to find and acknowledge what is there at this time. The focuser will come back in a moment to whatever has been set aside. If the focuser can't put an issue aside, you might suggest:

"Take a moment to dialogue with it, letting it know you recognize that it wants to be listened to right now, but that you need a few moments to get a little space from it in order to feel its priority along with some other things. You promise not to neglect it and will come back to it if it's really Number One, but for the time being would it be willing to sit down over there? *If this doesn't help in putting it aside, you might ask:* "Does this thing feel like it's the one that needs Focusing on right now, or does it feel like you could try again to set it aside and go further with the inventory?" *If it cannot be set aside, go to Step 3. If the person can set it aside, then say:* "Take a moment to notice what it feels like to have this whole thing set aside for the time being." *(Pause)*

C. Now ask yourself: "If I could leave this whole thing there for good and not need to carry it around ever again, would there be anything else between me and feeling really good right now?" Let me know if anything further surfaces.

> *If anything else comes, repeat (B) and (C) again and again, each time helping the focuser get a feel of all the things being set aside by changing the phrasing to:* "Now ask yourself: If I could leave both of these things (these three things, four, etc.) aside for good and not have to carry them around

again, would there be anything else between me and feeling really good? Let me know if something further surfaces, or if you can feel a reasonably open space now inside?" *Once the person has found such a space, continue with:*

D. Finally, take a few moments to notice whether there are a couple of other things in your life right now, not problems, that feel important to you . . . maybe a challenge, a dream, something you are looking forward to . . . something it would be good to identify. If you find anything like this, then set it aside next to your problems and let me know when you have done this.

> *The reason for this last question (D) is to allow an opportunity for the focuser to be in touch with more than negative things. Focusing is for all of life's issues, not just for problems. The Long Form Focusing inventory lets people identify everything that is important, positive, and negative. Step 2 then allows your body to set the priority of what needs to be focused on at this time. Sometimes, there's a surprise. A positive issue takes center stage.*

2. Feeling which one is Number One

> *The purpose of Step 2 is learning to trust the body's wisdom. Rather than thinking a priority with your mind, you attend not to the*

mental content, but to the body-feel of an issue. You're looking for the "feeling" doorway, not the "thinking" doorway. Often, you carry very serious life-issues, but the one with the most body-feel may be some inconsequential, irritating annoyance that won't let go inside. The point of Step 2 is to be drawn into your body knowing. That means you need to find the "feeling" thread into the tapestry of your inner life. When you have strong resistances to getting near a scary life-issue, your body will open another inner doorway for you—often through the body-feel of some lesser issue that will help you to be drawn inside. Once inside, your body eventually will guide you to the bigger issue, but in ways that allow you take one step at a time instead of being overwhelmed by it all.

Now, returning to whatever you have set aside, ask yourself: "Which one feels like it's Number One for me right now?" For example, which one feels the heaviest, hurts the most, has the most energy, is most exciting?" Say OK when you have found it or if you have difficulty finding it.

Again, note that the one Focusing asks him or herself which feels like Number One. The guide simply invites the focuser to check inside. The focuser is responding primarily to a question that he or she asks him or herself.

If the focuser has difficulty finding a Number One issue, or if two issues seem to have equal weight, you might ask if they would want to Focus on how it feels not knowing which is Number One. Or, you might inquire whether it would be all right to sit with the feeling of both issues together that seem to have equal importance. The body-feel of an issue is the important key to Focusing. Content is secondary. Help the focuser discover what stands out most prominently in a feeling way in all this. Once something has been found, then move on to Step 3.

3. Is it OK to be with this?

The purpose of Step 3 is to respect your defenses, not ignore or repress them. It is also to recognize that defenses and resistances are doorways, not walls, if you know how to be drawn through them. You'll know the answer to the question in Step 3 almost immediately. You'll either get a clear "Yes," or an ambiguous "Maybe," or a loud inner "No!" Often, we will feel significant resistance to getting near a scary inside place. This is our body telling us something. Instead of ignoring or repressing the feeling of resistance and trying to be with Number One, ask if it would be OK for a few moments to be caring and gentle with the feeling of "not wanting to get near this," "of wanting to run away," "of being scared at the prospect of looking at some dreaded inner place." The feeling of resistance has taken center stage. So, be with it and allow it to tell its story. More often than not, your resistance will provide a more effective doorway into your body knowing than will the Number One issue itself. Some resistances and issues may need what we call a "caring-feeling-presence." We'll say more about that in a moment.

Before going further, check for a moment to sense whether your body says it's OK to spend some time with this, giving it a more friendly hearing, allowing it to tell something of its story. Let me know whether this is OK or not.

If it's OK

If it is OK, but you don't know whether the issue might need caring-feeling-presence, ask:

Is this something between you and feeling good or is it something positive?

Then, if it is something between the focuser and feeling good, suggest ways you sense might be appropriate for creating a climate of caring-feel-ing-presence [cf. below] before going into Step 4. Be sure to end your suggestions with:

Let me know when you are ready to go further.

If it's not OK

If their response to the question, "Is it OK?" is "No," then say:

All right, ask yourself: "Is is OK to be with_____(fill in what the person has said—e.g., 'not wanting to get any place near it,' 'feeling too scared of it,' 'feeling it is too overwhelming to sit with,' etc.)? Let me know if it's OK to be with the feeling of all your resistance to getting near this issue.

If the answer is still "No," ask the focuser to check whether there may be some part of this whole thing that he or she could sit with. They may even need to go back to their inventory and select some less threatening issue. If that is necessary, you might ask how it feels not being able to face or be with a particular issue. Often, the feeling of resistance itself is the best doorway into Focusing. Work with the focuser to create a caring-feeling-presence before proceeding further.

Note: Caring-feeling-presence

For a more complete description of caring-feeling-presence, see E. McMahon, "How Can We Risk Owning What Is Real in Our Bodies?" in Beyond the Myth of Dominance: An Alternative to a Violent Society, Sheed & Ward 1993. *This chapter contains helpful examples and stories that are useful for understanding and teaching caring-feeling-presence.*

If, when leading someone, you can tell that the issue being worked with is difficult for them, quietly suggest something that helps create a **caring-feeling-presence** *so that it might be easier for them actually to let go into the body-feeling of the issue. Caring-feeling-presence means finding a different body way to be with stuck, resistant, scary inner feelings. Sometimes, it helps to be with them as "teacher" rather than "enemy." Perhaps you can hold them as you would hold a crying, hurting child. What will help you to have some kind of "kinship" with this place? For example, find a way that fits your temperament where you can imagine yourself putting your arm around the hurting place inside, rather than only having the body-feel of wanting to push it away.*

Remember, the purpose of a more open, caring, gentle inner climate or body-attitude is to help the focuser approach what is real inside, rather than reject, repress, ignore, or numb it with some "process-skipping" mechanism. There is a fine line here, so the guide needs to encourage the focuser whenever a caring-feeling-presence is used, to remain with the body-feelings in this climate of openness and availability in order to "own" these real feelings (difficult though they may be) rather than using the caring-feeling-presence as just one more form of "process-skipping," a substitute for being in touch with the truth of oneself.

Select one or two of the following suggestions, perhaps get feedback to discern if another is called for; allow time to do it; don't just read this page. Empathically, with the focuser, try to sense what is happening and adapt these suggestions creatively to his or her needs.

If this place inside feels so hurting, scary, stuck, or blocked that you want to run away from it, then take time to create an atmosphere of caring-feeling openness, gentleness, or kindness in a way that it can feel that presence from you. Perhaps hold and feel it in the same way you might hold and feel a crying, hurting child; or use some word or phrase to create a feeling climate toward it that is the opposite of the way you usually treat it. Maybe imagine putting your arm around it or patting it. Notice where you feel this issue most in your body and then, if feasible, put your hand there to comfort, pat, or caress it; or just let it know with your hand that you care and are there. You might want to try one or a combination of these approaches.

4. Letting go into it, just being in it, sensing the whole of it

Step 4 involves attending not to what your mind thinks about an issue but to how it feels in your body. Most of us want to play God and control the feelings that we don't like. Step 4 is allowing such feelings to be heard. Sometimes, you need caring-feeling-presence in order to do this. There is no way you can "think" the whole of an issue as it is carried in your body, but you can feel it. That's what Step 4 is about.

Now, ask yourself: "How does this whole thing feel in my body right now? How am I carrying it inside me?" Allow your awareness to seep into your body, to settle in and sense how all this feels inside. Say "OK" when you can feel something of this in your body.

The point of this last direction is to give you, the guide, feedback on whether a focuser with whom you are unfamiliar is or is not aware of body-feelings connected with whatever is being focused upon. Obviously, the suggestion is superfluous for a person who already experiences this connection or is successfully moving through the cycles of felt shifts.

Note that once the Focusing process is moving along and it becomes clear the focuser can

feel issues in his or her body, it is no longer nec-
essary to keep the directions for Steps 4 and 5
separate from one another. Steps 4 and 5 are
artificially separated in order to give the guide
feedback as to whether the one Focusing (pre-
sumably a beginner) can actually feel anything
in his or her body that is connected with what is
being focused upon. If it is clear the focuser has
a body-feel for what is being focused on, combine
the directions for Steps 4 and 5 together. For
example: "Take a moment to be with how all
that _____(insert whatever symbol has
been shared) feels, and then let me know if
something further comes that fits the way
this now feels as you sit with it."

5. Allowing it to express itself

Staying with the body-feel of an issue in Step 4,
sooner or later it will express itself in some
"symbol" that fits and feels right. The symbol
may be a word, a phrase, an image, a memory,
perhaps a feeling, tears, a giggle—anything
that comes and seems to "connect" in some way
with the issue being focused upon so there is
some easing or "felt rightness" about the con-
nection. Dr. Gendlin refers to such easing as a
"felt shift." This is the body's way of taking a
forward step toward wholeness in the resolu-
tion of an issue. Sometimes in Focusing there
can be a big felt shift. At other times, it is more
like a series of smaller steps, each contributing

*to forward movement. Focuser and guide need
to discern whether each smaller "step" needs to
go further at that time, or whether this is a stopping point for now.*

Now, staying with how this whole thing feels
inside, sense if anything further comes (like a
word or mental image, a memory or just some
other feeling) that connects with how it feels—
anything that resonates with or is on target
inside. Take your time and let me know if
something comes that fits the way this whole
thing feels.

*If a symbol comes, continue the process as
follows:*

A. *When a symbol is shared, let the focuser know that
his or her symbol has been heard by reflecting it
back exactly as spoken. If the focuser just nods or
says "OK," proceed to (B) and ask:*

B. Is this something that feels right to let unfold
a little further? *If the focuser says "No," and
wants to conclude his or her Focusing, go to Step
6. If the focuser says "Yes," and wants to continue,
go to (C).*

C. Ask yourself: "How does all this_____
(insert symbol if shared) now feel in my body?"
Take time to let go into and sense how all about
this feels inside and let me know if anything
further comes that fits the way this now feels.

Repeat Steps A, B, and C as long as the focuser wants to keep Focusing, or at least as long as you have time for this exercise.

Remember to repeat the suggestion to be caring and gentle with an issue whenever this might be helpful.

If the focuser comes to a bad feeling place that doesn't shift, or if they want to stop in a bad feeling place, try some of the following. Empathically work with the focuser, attempting to sense what is happening and adapt these suggestions creatively to his or her needs.

1. Ask yourself: "How does the worst of this feel in my body?"

2. Ask yourself: "What needs to happen (change) inside me for this whole thing to begin to feel better?"

3. Ask yourself: "What would feel like a small step forward with all this?"

4. Ask yourself: "What would feel like a breath of fresh air in this whole thing?"

5. Imagine, for a moment, how it would feel inside if this whole thing were all OK. *Pause to try to feel it.* Can you feel this way all the time? *If answer is "No" say:* Ask yourself, "What needs to change inside me for this to feel better?"

6. Staying with how this place feels inside, ask it: "What are you trying to do for me?" Let me

know if anything comes to answer this question. *Variation:* "How are you trying to help me?"

7. Ask this place inside: "How do you need me to be with you so you can tell me what you want?"

8. Would it be OK for a few moments to sit quietly and gently with not wanting to go further? *Then, if nothing comes, encourage the focuser with:* Leave this place inside promising that you will return at another time, letting it know that you respect its schedule, that you will check in again later to see whether it is ready to speak or still needs further nurturing.

9. As you get ready to stop, imagine taking this whole thing and putting it aside—on a shelf, or on the floor beside you, or in a bag. Notice what it feels like to do that, and just stay with this feeling for a few moments in an unhurried, quiet, gentle way before you stop. Let me know when you are ready to stop or if something connects that wants to go further at this time.

10. *Sometimes, when none of the above help, you might ask:* "Would it feel right to stop Focusing for a few moments and just talk a little about what you are feeling right now. We can go back to Focusing after talking a bit, if that is what you want to do."

   Then, you listen and reflect with "healing" or "active listening." You respond not just to the content that is shared, but to how the person feels inside when sharing this content. It can help to ask yourself: "How is this person in what he or she is saying?" Let the person know that you hear not just "what" they are saying, but "how they are in what they are saying—e.g., angry, lonely, sad, excited, confused." If during the course of this dialogue other felt senses appear, you can invite the focuser to check whether he or she might want to be with them in a Focusing way.

Finding out if it's OK to stop

Presuming the focuser has said nothing about stopping and you feel for various reasons—time, tiredness, your own feel of where he or she is at— that maybe this is the right place to conclude for now, we suggest the following approach:

Check inside and notice if this place needs to go further at this time or whether this is a place where it would be OK to stop, at least for now. Let me know what you find.

You follow along with the focuser's response, either continuing with A, B, C or going to Step 6, unless there is some serious reason not to. Notice that in the above wording, continuing is mentioned first and given priority over stopping, so you don't load your question in a way that might indicate you want to stop. If it seems that stopping is the priority, many focusers interpret this as an indication that the guide wants to stop. Focusers often then become distracted, not really paying attention to what their own felt sense is saying, or they become too inhibited to express it.

6. *Nurturing period*

Step 6 offers some quiet time in which to be aware of any change in how the body feels after having focused on an issue. This is a time for quiet reverence, thankfulness, perhaps marking special feeling places to which one might want to return at a later time. It is also a time for creating kinship with unfinished places that will need to be carried until the next Focusing, promising not to neglect them. For those who value the spiritual dimension of Focusing, this is a time for nurturing and being grateful for the body-sense of graced opening as difficult feeling places unfold into greater wholeness within the person.

Let's nurture this place with some "before and after checking" as we close. Take a few moments now to recall how it felt in your body when you began to Focus. *Allow a short pause for doing this.* Now, come to where you are inside at present, sensing whether this place feels the same as when you started or whether it has changed in any way. Let me know what you find.

If it does feel better

A. Before and after check

Noticing where in the body it has changed.

If the focuser indicates some change, then help him or her notice concretely where that difference is and how it feels in their body by suggesting:

Take a few moments to notice specifically in your body where there has been some change, like a loosening, releasing, easing.

Or, if this has been shared, use their earlier description of how the issue felt in their body when they began, as distinct from how it feels now.

Let me know what you find. *Pause and wait for feedback.*

B. Savoring the movement

If there has been some movement, you might say:

Now give yourself a little time to savor that movement, staying with whatever concrete change you can feel in your body. Take time to become familiar with the feel of this changed inner landscape so you can find your way back to it later. Perhaps, it might want to go further at another time or maybe you might want to return just to be nourished by the feel of this change. *Pause long enough for focuser to do this.*

C. Time to say thanks: grounding spiritual in the body

After you sense an appropriate period of quiet has been given for savoring, then:

CHRISTIAN EMPHASIS

If your orientation involves Christian spirituality or helping someone who values the Christian dimension of Focusing, you might very quietly and as unobtrusively as possible insert:

As you savor the feel of this movement toward more wholeness and healing, let yourself at the same time become aware that this is how God's grace feels physically in your body. *(Pause)* This is your unique body feeling of God's life-giving presence inside you—a presence and power of healing as real, as close, as tangible as you are willing to let yourself feel and reverence that change inside yourself. *(Pause)* In whatever way seems right, you might want to give yourself a few more moments just to be gratefully "in Christ" with all this. *(Pause)* Whenever you are ready, you can stop.

*For others, you might quietly suggest with as lit-
tle interruption as possible the following:*

As you savor the feel of this movement toward
wholeness and healing, in whatever way seems
right, give yourself a few more moments to be
grateful and reverent in this place of gift within
yourself—perhaps in a way that says, "Thank you."
(Pause) Whenever you are ready, you can stop.

If it does not feel better

*When something is stuck, blocked, going in cir-
cles, etc., help the focuser to be with how this feels
in a caring-feeling way, or listen to what it might
want to say as it is held gently. This often creates
an inner climate for it to speak. Therefore, when
whatever is being focused on feels the same, perhaps even worse, or maybe some easing but a
strong edge of unfinishedness that isn't OK, you
might suggest the following, slowly guiding with:*

Take a moment to let this place that feels so
_____ *(use their words, if possible)* know that
you hear it, that you are going to respect it and not
run away if it needs to tell you something. Being
present in this caring, open way, sense whether
anything comes that helps guide you toward
whatever is the right thing to do now. Let me
know if something comes. *Pause for feedback.*

If it says nothing, or you sense the focuser is scared and blocking and wants to stop, honor that by helping them conclude with something like the following:

As you bring this period of quiet to an end, let yourself feel as much of the unfinishedness in this whole thing as you can, asking it the question: "How do you need me to be with you so we can continue our journey together, so you can be my teacher rather than my enemy?" Let me know if anything comes that feels on target.

Even if this doesn't dispose the focuser for movement at that time, the attitude of remaining open to an unfinished place can tone the relationship for that possibility later on, because the question itself begins an inner reconciliation and usually feels more hopeful as a place to stop.

Further suggestions for guiding

1. Your primary role for guiding someone in Focusing is to help the focuser stay in the body-feel of his or her issue, and to create a trusting, caring, more secure climate within which it is easier to risk Focusing. The guide or companion creates this environment by the quality of presence in the relationship, one that is not hampered by the guide's need for control and success as a helper. Such an atmosphere encourages and disposes for Focusing and is, in

itself, a gift that heals and opens for further grace.

2. The nature of your response as a guide is not to make cognitive connections of insight but to support a forward movement of felt meaning within the focuser's body. This means your interventions should be intended to help an organismic process unfold. You're not there to **talk about** an issue, but to help the person stay in touch with **the body-feel** of that issue so it can tell its story.

3. Be ready to skip Steps 1 and 2 if the issue to be focused on is clearly evident. For example, something upsetting has just happened. **Always** check, though, to determine whether it is OK to be with this particular issue (Step 3), and if it needs to be held in a caring way before going further. Then, go through Steps 4–6.

4. Remember, the focuser cannot Focus while you (the guide) are talking or giving directions. Be mindful of brevity and clarity. Say what you have to say in order to support the process, then get out of the way and be quiet so the one Focusing can continue.

5. Always give clear ground rules so the one Focusing knows what to do next, and how to let you know when they have done what you asked. This frees the focuser to concentrate on Focusing and you from worrying about

whether it's evident how you are to be called upon if further input is needed.

6. If at any point you become unsure about what to do next, ask the one Focusing: "What does it feel right to do now?" If the answer is: "I don't know," then ask whether it would be OK just to sit with that feeling of unsureness for a while and sense whether anything comes from that.

7. The person Focusing is **always** the one in charge! If he or she wants to stop, stop! If such a person runs into something that is too scary to go further with and decides to back off, that's their choice. Let them back off. You, as guide, might suggest at that point something like: "Would it be all right just to be caring and gentle with the feeling of how scary this is becoming right now and the need to back away from it?" Help the person stay with whatever comes as a real felt meaning right now.

8. If you are running out of time you might ask, upon arriving at a natural resting place, "Check inside to see if this is something that needs to go further now, or would it be OK to stop here for the time being?" Generally, we find it better to weigh the option in favor of proceeding further with Focusing rather than abruptly injecting a stop sign. What you regard as a natural stopping place may not be such for the one Focusing.

9. Remember, while Focusing is always therapeutic, it is never a substitute for psychotherapy. The Focusing guide is a companion, not a therapist, unless professionally trained and licensed as well.

What to do if someone can't get a Felt Sense

When the focuser knows a problem with their mind but can't feel it in their body, we suggest the following:

1. Have such a person ask him or herself the following question, paying special attention to how their body responds: "I feel OK about this in my body, don't I?" *Allow time to do this then ask:* "Did you feel anything in your body that answered that? Just stay with this—be in it (Step 4), and see if something comes that connects with this feeling. Let me know if this happens."

2. Some people often have a **background feeling** that follows them around during the day. It is some way they always feel—sad, always rushing, feeling inferior to others, always trying so hard, etc. It often helps to focus on this background feeling.

3. Sometimes, it helps to pick two or three of the most important things the focuser has said if this person has talked about what is bothering

them. Look for the most **feeling** statements. This may be a single word or phrase. Tell the person: "When I say what I'm going to say, don't you say anything to me or to yourself, just be quiet and feel whatever comes." Then, slowly repeat the key words or phrases you have noted. Allow time for silence. If the person catches an edge of body-feeling, move into the next appropriate step.

4. Ask how the one Focusing feels about not being able to get hold of a felt sense.

5. Sometimes, when the one you assist seems to be getting nowhere, if it feels right invite them to stop Focusing and just talk about whatever they are trying to get close to. Respond with Healing Listening by reflecting how the person is in what he or she is saying, the body-feel that you pick up.

Don't engage in ordinary conversation in which you share your own opinions, comments, judgments, evaluations, etc. Rather, try to let the other person know that you hear how the issue feels in them, or if you can't catch any feeling, at least reflect each point being made.

When doing Healing Listening you might find it helpful to ask **yourself** the following question: "How is this other person in what he or she is saying?" What you seek to become aware of is not merely the **content** being shared—**what** is talked about—but, rather, **how this person must be feeling inside the experience he or she narrates.**

Scared, angry, upset, etc. You, as healing listener, then respond not to **what** is talked about, but to **how** this individual feels in what is talked about. Let the other person know that you hear their excitement, desperation, loneliness, frustration, jealousy, etc.

Then, when both of you catch the edge of some more prominent feeling that may arise during such sharing, you might ask: "Is that something that feels right to focus on?" If the answer is "Yes," then ask: "Does it need some caring presence before going further? Let me know when you are ready to move further." Then, guide into Steps 4 and 5, when they are ready.

Remember, the greatest gift we give to someone whom we accompany in Focusing is a caring presence that is non-manipulative. Technique can be very helpful, but in the long run is of little consequence if this presence is missing. Such presence enables the focuser to feel safe enough to own whatever is real in his or her body. Your own body-experience of what Focusing feels like from the inside, plus your body-feel for the "felt shift," as well as having acquired a body-sense for how to create a "caring-feeling-presence" toward your own fears and hurts, will give you the most essential knowledge you need to guide in Focusing— even if you make technical mistakes.

Our experience is that when people feel accompanied and not manipulated, this is such a disposing grace that if the above body-learnings have been acquired through your own Focusing, then they give you the on-target directions you need to support the process. It seems that when this presence and this body-wisdom come into a relationship, the process takes care of itself, despite our other shortcomings.

APPENDIX 2

Process-Skipping: A block to the body-life of Spirit

Peter A. Campbell, Ph.D.

I can still see her face as I walked out of the retirement center twenty years ago. Frightened. Unsure of the future. Pleading with her eyes for her only son not to leave. Yet, with a stiff British reserve firmly in place and a voice assuring me that everything would work out well for her. Indeed, it has, for my mother could not have received better care during the intervening years. But the personal inner struggle triggered by that experience led me on a journey through unimagined dimensions of my own inner world—unowned aspects of my experience that at the time I scarcely knew even existed.

What I discovered was a vivid personal experience of my own addictive process and the precise psychological mechanism that locked this compulsive pattern in place, making it so resistant to change. I want to share something of this experience, reflecting on it with you because what I am learning from my own body's wisdom may provide a key for you and others who struggle with similar issues of addiction, intimacy, and growth in the Spirit.

When I walked out of the retirement center I felt bad. But that bad feeling was nothing compared to the guilt that surfaced two or three weeks and several phone calls later. Finally, I couldn't take it any more and went to visit my mother. The guilt ceased for a time. But soon would come a phone call or anniversary and the familiar pattern repeated itself. Guilt inevitably returned. Fairly soon a predictible sequence became evident, not to me, but to those who knew and loved me. Something would trigger feelings of guilt about my mother being alone in the retirement center and my response, in order to alleviate the guilt, would be to go to visit her.

I never took time to sit with my guilt, to wonder about or listen to it. I simply reacted. GUILT—go visit mother. In fact, I soon became addicted to visiting mother as a way to handle my guilt. Some people use alcohol to "deal with" or deaden such feelings. Others have such an overpowering "need to please" that they fall into all kinds of addictive behaviors as a way to ease inner pain, insecurity, and confusion.

Gendlin makes it clear that the direction toward a felt sense is always into and through the feeling, never away from it. Yet, for me, every time I felt guilt, I moved in the opposite direction, trying to "deal with it" by visiting my mother. I skipped right past the point of entry into my own process. I quite literally became addicted to visiting my mother as a way to control the feeling of guilt. I substituted this activity in place of entering through the emotion into the felt sense of it all and allowing my untold story to unfold.

I remember a friend once telling me that when her children were in a sixth grade class on drug abuse, the teacher had asked for comments on how they dealt with difficult feelings. The responses were frank, honest, and for the future well being of our society, a bit unsettling. "I listen to music." "I run." "I phone my friends." "I go to the refrigerator." "I shop." "I go to my computer." The litany was quite creative, and the potential for addictive escape enormous. Each child had already found his or her way to numb, to distract, to escape, to avoid coming to grips with and owning how they really felt inside their body. They didn't learn this by themselves. They simply watched the adults around them and modeled their behavior on what they saw.

If I had children of my own, my behavior would surely have reenforced this same futile pattern of avoidance in them as well. Right at the threshold of my own body feeling of guilt I took a direction that made some form of addiction inevitable. I substituted visiting my mother in place of being in touch with how my body carried the uncomfortable feelings that no one had ever taught me how to be with when I was a child. Psychological addiction involves a *substitution* of one behavior, feeling or attitude in place of another, rather than becoming congruent with, owning, and *processing* what is real, thereby allowing it to unfold and tell its story so the body-feel of it can be carried in a different way.

People make this same tragic choice every day of their lives in situations far more complex than the simple example I am sharing. But the psychological process remains the same. We seek to control the "bad feeling" to make it go away or to substitute something better in its place. In the course of doing this, however, we fall prey to the very psychological mechanism of escape that we have stumbled into or perhaps deliberately chosen. It soon becomes our jailer, locking an addictive pattern in place. Every time I came near to the doorway of guilt and could feel those unpleasant stirrings in my body, I was whisked away to a temporary soothing of these feelings (through a visit to my mother) and the doorway to permanent change remained tightly shut. The untouched treasure of potential transformation in my body's way of carrying guilt remained nothing more than a hidden possibility. My guess is that such potential is rarely touched in the many lives of desperation where addictive confusion leads people away from their bodies—away from the true home of their own spirit!

Most people, in my experience, at one time or other use religion and their relationship to God as just one more way of numbing and escape. I certainly did for many years. But it does not have to be this way. I am writing these words because I know from personal experience that there is an alternative.

We can now put a label on the pattern that locked my addictive experience in place and made it so resistant to change. It is called a *process-skipping structure*. This is a phrase chosen by Dr. Eugene Gendlin, who developed Focusing.[1] The label, of course, can never help us to change, but the understanding it brings can alert us to where in our experience we must look for our own process-skipping structures.

Psychological addiction develops because people have feelings they don't like, and they don't know how to be with those feelings in a way that allows them to change. A process-skipping structure, like visiting my mother, is substituted in place of the body-process of real change—and the substitute soon becomes our prison.

Process-skipping structures are not just obvious things like drugs, alcohol, sex, work, or pleasing other people. Prayer, meditation, volunteer work, anything that can be substituted for a congruent owning of what is real inside me contains the negative potential for contributing to a process-skipping pattern of addiction.

Any religious exercise, any form of meditation, any "growth" practice that takes me away from the truth of myself as this is carried in my body and substitutes, instead, some more acceptable feeling or attitude in place of what is real—that practice or exercise or prayer, if engaged in for some time, will inevitably become addictive.

Most of us are well trained to learn with our minds. Few of us know how to learn from our bodies. Focusing teaches us a special way to be *in* our guilt, or whatever other feelings need to be heard, without trying to fix any of them. If we remain with this non-verbal resonance in our bodies long enough, without trying to force the mind's meaning upon it, sooner or later it will speak and symbolize itself—often in surprising ways. A word will come, an image, a memory will bubble to the surface, perhaps tears or a delighted giggle at some felt humor in the seriousness of it all. And when the connection is made, when the symbol fits, something inside says, "Yes," and eases in our body's feel about the whole thing. We notice that now it feels different—a difference that is lighter, or more loose. It is less painful or scary to carry inside.

From that point forward, your felt carrying of that issue is never again the same. You may still need to take further steps. Other aspects of the issue may yet remain to be heard. But your body has been gifted with some kind of loosening. The ice has thawed and cracked a little. The floes break up and begin to float once more. Movement starts to happen, meaning begins to unfold.

What becomes so painful for many of us is when the feeling of being blocked remains stuck. That is where burnout and breakdown occur. But if there is some body-sense that movement has occurred, then hope rises anew. It's amazing how much unfinished stuff we can live with when we sense it is on the way toward being resolved in our bodies.

I certainly know I felt this in the gradual unfolding of my own guilt. When I finally took time to create a caring presence around this negative feeling and not just react in an addictive way, my incomplete story began to unfold. There was deep anger and resentment over unfinished issues in childhood—separation because of war and illness over which my parents had no control. But I still felt these absences and the pain of them. The resentments were deep inside, still carried in a body way. My mind had arrived at its own adult peace and understanding. But my body was still seven years old.

How little we understand the process of human wholeness. Our mind seeks *solutions*. It wants answers, information, facts. Our bodies, on the other hand, seek *resolution* in the way they carry painful or even joyful experiences. If there is no resolution, then we go to our graves tense and dissatisfied.

Focusing provides a simple, practical way in which to be gifted with our own body resolution. That's what makes this process so different. The goal is not analysis—acquiring more information, finding out what's wrong with us, or simply getting in touch with feelings. All such busyness still leaves us with the troublesome question: "Then what?" Focusing teaches us how to be with our body's consciousness in a way that allows it to speak to us. Then, change happens in how we carry feelings and in other ways our body tries to communicate with us.

I was taught a vivid lesson about this one evening when taking a quiet stroll. I noticed a small, stuffed ball lying next to the road. Picking it up, I continued my walk, idly tossing and catching the ball. I was struck by how rarely I had taken time in my adult years for this simple boyhood pleasure.

Frequently, my toss was off and I'd need to run a bit to catch the ball. It was then that I became very aware of something—a consistent pattern. As I tossed the ball and it fell back toward me, I would follow with my eye until it was about a foot from my hand and then, suddenly, my eyes would veer away in the last split second before the ball actually came into my grasp. "Keep your eye on the ball." The words came back from grammar school baseball experiences—but this time I really heard them. For the next several moments I was very conscious of disciplining myself to watch the ball fall all the way into my hand. I could sense a different body-feel in the experience. When my eyes veered away, there was a feel of flinching— an avoidance. But when I followed the ball all the way into my hand, I noticed a kind of newness, something fresh—like I had never done this before.

Then I fell into one of those precious moments of reverie where things began falling together and my experience took on a meaning far more significant than what appeared in this idle pastime. Not only did it reveal a great deal about myself, it offered a fresh perspective on my life's work.

Most people know that they have feelings. *What they don't know is how to follow those feelings all the*

way into their body whenever they need to change!
Like my eyes following the ball, most of us veer
off at the last moment, rarely experiencing the
newness of what it's like when such feelings can
change and unfold from the inside.

*Focusing is a simple, easily learned process that will
help you to follow a feeling all the way into your body.*
It is a potential key to unlock even the most stub-
born patterns of psychological addiction. Then we
can freely listen to our own spirit as the story
unfolds from inside.

The difference Focusing made for me was strik-
ing. When addictively visiting my mother, I was
invariably there to get the monkey of guilt off my
back. I fulfilled a duty. But I was rarely present to
my mother with that deeper communication and
sharing wherein there is true companionship. I'm
sure mother felt this in some way. But, as I have
taken time and begun allowing guilt to unfold, I
find that mother and I are becoming friends. We
share a great deal, have much in common, and are
blessed with a similar sense of humor. It is a wonderful gift, finally, to discover your parent as a
friend.

Now, let's go one step further in our understanding of process-skipping.

The emerging world of Felt Sense

Many years ago people routinely died of something
they called "consumption." It was an ominous

word covering what we now know could have been anything from cancer to tuberculosis. Given the limited knowledge at that time, one word was used to cover a multitude of maladies.

We face much the same situation today with our very limited traditional distinction between "thinking" and "emotion." "Emotion" is a word much like "consumption." It is a generic title for the teeming world of body knowing that we have only recently begun to understand. The average person can differentiate physical sensations like sweaty palms, dizziness, and palpitations from emotions like anger, loneliness, and love. But that's about as far as our everyday ability to differentiate goes. At least it was until Eugene Gendlin came along to open for us the world of what he called the "felt sense."

> A felt sense is not just an emotion. Fear, anger, joy, sadness—these are emotions. A felt sense is different, it is global and fuzzy. It includes more than the emotion—many things, most of them not clearly known. It is a bodily quality, like heavy, sticky, jumpy, fluttery, tight. At first it has no fitting label . . .
>
> Let me show the difference between an emotion and a felt sense. Anger is an emotion. When you are angry, you recognize that. No puzzle, nothing vague, you're mad. But if you relax a little, you can sense: "There is more involved in the whole thing." For example, you may sense a breathless, hurried quality, a

sense that you'd like to stay mad—you don't want to stop and see that you're a little wrong. That uneasy quality has no name of its own. Where would you find that? Under the anger, in it, around it, at the edge of the anger. But words like "edge" do not describe it literally . . .

You can sense that it has a life of its own if you try to talk yourself out of it. It will resist. If you say something about it, and then attend back to the felt sense, you can sense that what you said is wrong. Yet you don't know what would be right to say. You cannot control when it opens. Something comes directly from it when it opens. Or perhaps you accidentally thought something right, and it opens in response.

A felt sense is unmistakably meaningful, and yet we don't know what it is. In contrast we know the emotions when we have them.[2]

Eugene Gendlin has probed further into the world of body-knowing and helped us realize that within every emotion is a broader kind of body-sense that he named the felt sense. We generally don't have easily available words or concepts to describe this little recognized aspect of body knowing. It's more like your body sense of "all about this relationship" without going into specifics and details.

If you stop for a moment to reflect upon the experience of someone you love, you may notice

that your body-sense of them can be simultaneously both warm and cuddly as well as irritated
and annoyed. Your body knowing of someone
you love is really quite complex. Attention may be
focused on the current emotion of the moment.
But at the same time, your body simultaneously
holds all your other dimensions of *feltness* about
this relationship.

Why is this important? Because just as its useful
to know whether someone has tuberculosis or
cancer, so too, it helps to locate and understand
what is happening inside our body knowing. This
is especially true in the light of what Gendlin has
discovered, namely, that feelings are able to
change within the person to the extent that he or
she can be in touch with more than emotion. That
is, they must be able to discern and own the felt
sense. Potential for change and growth lies in the
felt sense, not in the emotion! If all you do is feel
and re-feel emotions, you will just go around in
circles or wallow in feeling. Merely feeling a
painful emotion over and over again provides
absolutely no assurance that it will ever change
into something better!

Being able to remain in touch with a felt sense in
a way that allows it to unfold and tell its story is
the key to any lasting forward movement in the
emotions connected with that felt sense. Gendlin
deserves great credit for uncovering the felt sense.
But, equally important, he also found that we
have our own unique and highly developed "process-skipping" ways of remaining out of touch
with this vital reservoir of human knowing.

"Process-skipping structures" and the "felt sense" together provide a psychological framework for evaluating many of the so-called "spiritual" practices that foster addiction within religion. Let me give you an example from a Christian book on prayer.

Spiritualities of control

There are spiritualities and spiritual exercises that can best be described as spiritualities of control. They easily become part of our arsenal of process-skipping devices. They protect us from change and, therefore, become a piece of the system that firmly locks addictive patterns in place. Their goal is not process but containment—the polar opposite of a healthy openness to grace.

Let's consider an example that might at first appear to be an effective prayer for healing anger and bitterness over past hurt. I want to point out the negative, process-skipping, addictive potential in this prayer. Then, I want to reflect on how it might have been experienced in a way that could lead toward inner wholeness rather than repression or neglect of what is real in our body.

The prayer in question appears in a book by Eddie Ensley, *Prayer That Heals Our Emotions*.[3] Ensley quotes from Anthony de Mello's book *Sadhana*,[4] and begins by having you relax and recall scenes from your past where you were hurt by someone. He invites you to imagine taking the offending person by the hand and telling him or her that you forgive them. The exercise continues as follows:

> Each time you use this prayer experience, you can imagine different scenes and different people.
>
> As some of the people pass before your mind's eye you will feel uncomfortable telling them, "I forgive you." The hurts are held so deeply that it is difficult for you to let go of them. Father Anthony de Mello, in his . . . book, *Sadhana*, . . . suggests the following way of letting go of deep hurt and unforgiveness.
>
> First, imagine that you see Jesus Christ on the cross. Take whatever time you might need to have a sense of Him on the cross.
>
> Now turn to the scene of pain where you are hurt and stay with that scene for a while. Keep alternating between the picture of Jesus on the cross and the scene of your hurt. Soon you will find your resentment slipping away from you, and a feeling of peace and joy will sweep over you. A feeling of lightheartedness will overcome you as the image of Our Lord on the cross enables you to let go of imbedded hurt.[5]

I am uncomfortable with this prayer exercise for three reasons. First, I always become ill at ease when someone describes a practice and then tells me *in advance* how I am going to feel after I have performed it! Second, this particular exercise has the negative potential of shaming with guilt. "Jesus died on the cross for you as well as for the one who did you wrong—and you still won't forgive this person?" But even more negligent and misleading, in my view, is the fact that absolutely no attempt is made to enter into, to own, and process one's anger. Instead, feelings of compassion and love for Jesus on the cross are deliberately cultivated in order to override and subdue, to smooth and soothe away the negative emotion of anger.

In short, feelings of compassion and love are *substituted* in place of feelings of anger. The anger in no way is owned. The deeper felt sense is neither heard nor allowed to express itself. Unprocessed anger is pushed down for a time—only to reemerge whenever another occasion arises that provokes the memory of all such unfinished business.

When this occurs, as inevitably it must, the prayer exercise and feelings of compassion for Jesus on the cross will need to be repeated once again in order to control this troublesome resurgence. Soon, a predictable and addictive scenario of process-skipping prayer will be born, just like I used visiting my mother to exorcise my demon of guilt. The bottom line in all this is that the anger will never change. It will just go on repeating itself over and over again until, finally, it is owned and the body's felt sense is allowed to unfold.

Having said all this, what might have been a healthy way to present such prayer—one that could preserve a familiar and cherished prayer form while at the same time incorporating sound common sense that would keep us in touch with the truth of ourselves?

If Jesus could be an encouraging presence, accompanying the person as he or she enters into and owns real inner feelings, then this could be a prayer that leads toward healing and wholeness. Here, there is no avoiding or denying what is real. There is an openness to the surprise of grace working at the heart of what we fear or avoid most inside ourselves.

This approach stands in stark contrast to our earlier example. There, the experience of Jesus actually pulls the one at prayer away from his or her real anger by substituting, instead, feelings of compassion and love in its place. Nothing of the anger ever really gets processed! The person is being "set up" for addictive prayer. In our second example, the person in prayer draws upon a resource (Jesus), whose life and presence strengthen that person's resolve to enter into their own dark and frightening body feelings wherein lies a potential for grace and healing.

Eugene Gendlin could not have said it more eloquently and simply: "Every 'bad' feeling is potential energy toward a more right way of being if you give it space to move toward its rightness."[6] The surprise of grace waits at the core of what we often use prayer to run from and avoid inside ourselves. The body-life of Spirit yearns to unfold within the as yet unheard story of my anger and the hurt that sustains it. The prayer addict misses all this. An overriding need for control closes down openness to grace! Such persons become as psychologically addicted to using Jesus on the cross to manipulate their anger as others might use work, drugs, or alcohol as a means of escape.

I know this will be difficult for some to accept, because they view prayer as good and drugs as bad. But the same negative potential for escape exists in the area of religious practice as well—perhaps even more so—because it is socially acceptable to pray, whereas it is frowned upon to become a drug addict.

But is the prayer addict any better off, or any less destructive in passing on an addictive pattern of escape to the next generation? We need more public awareness and discussion of the latent addictive power that lies in religion when it is abused by persons whose need for escape or security is so great that they will use anything to control their feelings.

Five criteria for evaluating spiritual and growth practices

Let me close by sharing five criteria that have helped us to evaluate spiritual/growth practices.

(1) Does the practice support you in owning your feelings, or does it merely make you aware of emotions without helping them to be in process? Just because you know you're mad doesn't

mean you know how to move toward some better way of being inside yourself. As Gendlin says, "Knowing is not the process of changing!"

(2) Does the practice keep you in touch with your own feelings in a way that allows them to unfold, or does it try to substitute other more acceptable feelings in place of those that are troublesome?

(3) Is the practice one that actually facilitates change in the feeling of some issue in your body, or does it merely provide you with information that affects your ideas and thinking about that issue?

(4) Is the practice one that achieves its effect in you through self-engineering and control or through self-surrender in openness to a process of grace?

(5) When using a practice to grow beyond stuck feelings, is the level of positive change that occurs in the way an issue feels in your body something that endures after the exercise, or must you keep repeating the practice in order to maintain the level of change that happens?

Appendix 3

From whom should I learn Bio-Spiritual Focusing?

Edwin M. McMahon, Ph.D.

It makes a big difference who first introduces you to Focusing as well as with whom you continue to focus if you are going to develop a body-feel for the intrinsic spirituality in this process. Focusing that will uncover this potential should be experienced with a guide who:

a) is free enough to journey empathically with you, not direct, manipulate, or control your process from their perspective or needs;

b) doesn't need to have you succeed in Focusing in order to feel good about him or herself;

c) knows the process from the inside as gift; that is, has a body-feel for the grace dimension of this process;

d) regularly Focuses him or herself

If the body-feel for this process, as well as its gift dimension, is not maturing in the person guiding you, especially in the beginning, Focusing can easily turn into just one more self-help gimmick, even if the guide does not become manipulative. If the profound spirituality that Focusing can reveal is ever to mature in us, this process must be taught and shared in a way that experientially lays a foundation for a new "graced" quality of relationship to ourselves, to one another, and the world around us.

Over and over again, Focusing must be experienced in our body as honoring the role of grace within whatever is real in human life. This is the very basis for caring—toward self, others, and the planet. The last thing any of us need to be taught are more techniques of control. This outworn approach is already so deeply embedded and reinforced by our cultural conditioning that only the constant, repeated body experience of the exact opposite actually working can begin to change such programming with an alternative. Ideas or explanations about an alternative are simply inadequate. They change nothing in the body.

Therefore, when you choose a Focusing guide to introduce you to this process, or when you make a Focusing program, try to learn in an atmosphere that lays this experiential foundation for spirituality. The resource lies within your guide's experience of Focusing as grounded in grace. That person or those persons must clearly have a body-sense for some Power greater than their own controlling talents, expertise, or knowledge of the process. They must clearly acknowledge and experientially support the presence of this gifting Power as the key factor that "allows Focusing to work."

One of the best ways to evaluate a Focusing program is by talking to someone you know who has this sensitivity and has been in the sessions. Another is to watch the Focusing guide in action on videotapes, if they are available. What you want to look for is whether the guide is merely taking the Focuser through the steps of this process or, whether there is accompaniment in helping the Focuser recognize and honor whatever symbols come as gift, taking time to pause and nurture the physical feel of grace within whatever movement occurs in the body. Does the guide demonstrate an "inside" appreciation for the gift dimension of this journey and open this up to the Focuser, suggesting that he or she take time to savor it, get the body-feel of it, and be in it in a way that says "thank you" as they conclude the Focusing session?

Focusing can mature the body knowing of gratitude in us as we physically feel change, if the guide supports our savoring and nurturing this movement. Feelings of helplessness, frustration, terror, grief, shame, etc., that seem hopelessly stuck and then change during Focusing, can provide a profound body experience of our utter dependence on gift if, once again, the guide is sensitive in suggesting time to feel the giftedness of this healing.

Focusers need support in learning how to sense the sacred within all that is real in their lives, especially in what we label as "bad," because by

"owning" what we have been taught to "disown"
in our bodies we discover the gifted movement of
change and healing. We all need to experience this
over and over again until it finally begins to sink
in. The Focuser needs help in order to reverence
and listen to whatever is real in his or her body.
This is the only starting point for change and spiritual growth. At times this starting point may be
the terror of Focusing itself, or simply your not
having the energy, or feeling too unsupported to
Focus at all.

It can never be emphasized too much that
whatever your body tells you is real, is your starting
point and sacred territory because it is an invitation
for grace. A sense of its sacredness and potential as
a place for gift helps you learn how to care for
yourself, and especially for the feelings you often
label as "unspiritual." We all want to manipulate
and fix those "bad" feelings in ourselves and others. Only through the guide, whose sense for the
presence of gift in all that exists is maturing, can
this attitude break through and rub off on the
Focuser, toning the feel one gets for the spirituality in Focusing. *Guides need to know this in their own
bodies in order to pass it on to others.* If you have any
experience of what I am trying to describe, it will
not take long for you to discern who has such
knowledge from the "inside" and who does not.

If this is new territory for you, then there are
externals you can look for as signposts. The way
in which Focusing steps are taught and how one is
led in Focusing should always clearly convey:

a) That the one Focusing is in charge. The guide only suggests and invites the focuser to check out something, leaving the focuser to make his or her own decisions. The guide is not trying subtly to "fix" the focuser.

b) That the symbols given in Focusing are gifts (graces), not something we do to ourselves or make happen.

c) That the focuser is being supported in creating a body disposition of open, patient waiting, and listening so crucial for a prayerful, contemplative posture in which the gift of the symbol may be received.

d) That the way Focusing is taught clearly conveys no encouragement to bring in religious symbols (like Jesus, Mary, saints, etc.) as a way to "make" hurting or scary issues feel better. Rather, the focuser is supported in honoring a religious symbol as one would honor any symbol that might emerge spontaneously during Focusing, while at the same time carefully checking with his or her body to sense whether or not that religious symbol really *feels* connected, not just "thinks" connected. In other words, the focuser is helped to discern whether a "felt shift" in how the body carries the issue being focused on has actually occurred in connection with the religious symbol or not. The reason for this caution is that many religious people have been taught to bring in religion as a way to "disown" what they really feel in their bodies, thereby short-circuiting the very feelings that need to be "owned" and healed with God's grace. In Focusing language, this is called "process-skipping," and sets people up for an addictive use of religion.

In summary then, what you look for in a Bio-Spiritual Focusing guide or teacher is someone who helps you to "own" whatever your body tells you is real. This is a person who helps you create an inner climate of openness and waiting so you may receive the gift of whatever symbol connects with your body's felt sense, bringing change in the way an issue then feels. Focusing, as well as the relationship between you and your guide, is a gifted, bio-spiritual process of wholeness. It is a relationship in which both the focuser and guide honor and reverence whatever is real in the focuser's life, allowing symbols to be given as gift, rather than using any techniques that would convey or create a climate of fixing, manipulating, or making something happen. Focusing is taught as a "disposing" for grace, an inner body-climate that opens the focuser to receive these symbols.

This emphasis then influences:

a) the wording of the steps;

b) the use and wording of any interventions;

c) the attitude of both focuser and guide toward the whole process;

d) the quality of presence of the guide and his or her perception of their role;

e) the openness of the guide *to grow as well in the relationship* by relinquishing a controlling responsibility toward the focuser;

It also supports:

f) maturation in the "art of waiting," deepening a body-feel for living in the rhythm of grace, rather than of one's own agenda all the time;

g) growing in the ability to care for and learn from our brokenness instead of relating to it as an "enemy" to be manipulated and forced into change;

h) and finally, provides the focuser with experience of a new paradigm for community.

Focusing learned with this emphasis on a body-feel for grace reveals the basis for community not founded on dominance. It teaches this because we experience that both inner and outer community are given as gift when we risk empowerment in mutual vulnerability.

Appendix 4

Ten learnings from Bio-Spirituality that draw us into a global spirituality

Edwin M. McMahon, Ph.D.

1. The human body is a common doorway of awareness through which all people can pass in order to move beyond conflicting ethnic, religious, social, and political differences. Such differences are based upon diverse interpretations, histories, attitudes, and cultures. Divisive interpretations are not *solved* rationally but *resolved* experientially through forward movement into a further dimension of the body's knowing.

2. Once inside our body knowing, we discover that it has a special wisdom and intelligence.

3. There is a simple way for all of us to enter into what our body knows. It is called Bio-Spiritual Focusing.

4. Through Bio-Spiritual Focusing we can be encouraged to notice a rich tapestry of common human feeling that emerges around the unfolding process of felt-sensing.

5. Today, different areas of research converge to indicate that these feelings are part of a global, experiential reservoir of human body knowing at the felt-sensing level.

6. Bio-Spiritual Focusing invites and encourages us to dip into this reservoir, broadening our Focusing beyond problem solving and crisis management. We can allow feelings to form felt senses that speak to us of the vast wisdom that our body knows.

7. Through such experience, the barriers between us and a Larger Body that surrounds and penetrates us can begin to fade as a common body knowing tells us that we all exist within One Body and its Gifting Process. A common human bond can then emerge.

8. When reflecting together from within this common body knowing, two basic experiences stand out prior to any interpretation: (1) That we all exist in One Body, and (2) That it is a Gifting Process. With this common experience to unite us, why don't we use it as the basis for reflection and dialogue together in the fashioning of a global spirituality? We are taking a first step with Bio-Spiritual Focusing,

using our body knowing as the bridge into further reflection.

9. This is a gigantic leap in evolution—the realization that our common self-reflection is the Self-reflection of a Larger Body.

10. Out of such experience, a global spirituality together with communities and a common identity in the One Gifting Process can be born.

Notes

Preface

1. Carl G. Jung, *Psychology and Religion: West and East*, Collected Works, Vol. 2 (New York: Pantheon, 1958), p. 537.

Introduction

1. Pierre Teilhard de Chardin, *The Future of Man*, translated from the French by Norman Denny (New York: Harper & Row, 1964), p. 90.

2. Eugene T. Gendlin, revised instructions to *Focusing*, 2nd ed. (New York: Bantam Books, 1981).

3. Pierre Teilhard de Chardin, *The Phenomenon Of Man* (New York: Harper & Brothers Publishers, 1959), pp. 284–85.

4. Abraham H. Maslow, *Religions, Values, and Peak Experiences* (Columbus: Ohio State University Press, 1964), pp. 11, *xiv, xiii.*

Chapter 2

1. Gendlin, *Focusing*.

2. Ibid., p. 77.

Chapter 4

1. Teilhard de Chardin, *The Phenomenon of Man*, p. 311.

2. Michael Murphy, *Jacob Atabet—A Speculative Fiction* (Millbrae, Calif.: Celestial Arts, 1977).

Chapter 5

1. Alan Watts, *The Book—On the Taboo Against Knowing Who You Are* (New York: Pantheon Books, 1966), p. 11.

Chapter 6

1. Gendlin, *Focusing*, p. 77.

Chapter 7

1 Teilhard de Chardin, *The Future of Man*, p. 280.

2. William James, *The Varieties of Religious Experience* (New York: The New American Library, a Mentor Book, 1958), p. 388.

3. Dom Sebastian Moore, *God Is a New Language* (Westminster, Md.: Newman Press, 1967), p. 54.

4. Karl Rahner, "Christology and an Evolutionary World View," in *Theology Digest*, vol. 28, no. 3, fall 1980, p. 211.

5. Sir Arthur Eddington as quoted by David Foster in *The Intelligent Universe—A Cybernetic Philosophy* (New York: G. P. Putnam's Sons, 1975), pp. 164–65. Mr. Foster is quoting from Sir Arthur Eddington's remarks in *The Nature of the Physical World* (London: J. M. Dent and Sons Ltd., 1935).

Chapter 8

1. Carl G. Jung, *Modern Man in Search of a Soul*, translated by W. S. Dell and Cary F. Baynes (New York: Harcourt, Brace & World, Inc., a Harvest Book, 1963; first published in 1933), p. 235.

2. Ibid., p. 219–20.

3. Jung, *Psychology and Religion: West and East*, p. 535–37.

4. Gregory Baum, *Man Becoming: God in Secular Experience* (New York: Herder & Herder, 1970), p. 264.

5. Maslow, *Religions, Values, and Peak Experiences*, p. *xiv*.

Appendix 2

1. Gendlin, *Focusing*.

2. Eugene T. Gendlin, *Let Your Body Interpret Your Dreams* (Wilmette, Ill.: Chiron Publications 1986), p. 52–53.

3. Eddie Ensley, *Prayer That Heals Our Emotions* (Columbus: Contemplative Books, 1986).

4. Anthony de Mello, S.J., *Sadhana: A Way to God* (St. Louis: The Institute of Jesuit Sources, 1978).

5. Ensley, *Prayer that Heals our Emotions*, pp. 74–75.

6. Gendlin, *Focusing*, p. 75.

The Institute for Bio-Spiritual Research

The Institute is an international network of several thousand people—parents, counselors, health care providers, hospice volunteers, clergy and sisters, teachers, therapists, retreat house staffs, and spiritual guides—in fact, anyone dedicated to peacemaking through human wholeness. We believe this approach involves taking the actual body-steps that invite the gift dimension of life (grace) to unfold within ourselves and in our relationships with others. Through Bio-Spiritual Focusing we take time to open our body's awareness (not just our mental processes), so that we may experience a "body-feel" for the giftedness of life and the deep inner and spiritual connection of all things.This is what we mean by a body- or Bio-Spirituality.

Our organization is not affiliated with any church, political party, country, or vested interest. We are a member supported, shared leadership network of peacemakers from the inside. Through our "Levels courses," publications, videotapes, retreats, and Six Day Intensives we share very practical, teachable skills and attitudes that help us to live a peacemaking process in our daily lives.

The following values and goals tie us together as a worldwide network seeking ways to empower healthy spiritual growth and leadership.

1. Continually trying to develop more effective growth processes as alternatives to the violent ways we are taught to treat ourselves, others, and our environment.

2. Seeking to develop a global/environmental spirituality grounded in the "body/Body" that we all share.

3. Creating a body-spirituality that will help both adults and children to grow beyond the need for drugs and other destructive addictions.

4. Supporting the production of video, audio, and printed resources that can assist the Institute in reaching out to more diverse groups with Bio-Spiritual Focusing.

5. Sharing our conviction with parents, teachers, religious leaders, and others that children today desperately need a "body-feel" for the reality of what most of us call "God" and "grace." They need this experience as an alternative to relationships and systems all around them that they no longer see working. We believe in introducing youngsters to their own body-experience (not just "talk" and "rules")

of being connected in some "Larger Body" and gifting (graced) process. This experience must be discovered as integral to the development of their own self-esteem, positive self-identity, and responsibility toward the entire global body. Only by discovering such a valuing process within themselves will they ever realize how community as well as common moral and social values can be nurtured in a pluralistic, multi-religious society.

Information about membership in the Institute, its programs, as well as a list of audio, video, and written resources on Bio-Spiritual Focusing may be obtained by writing:

Institute for Bio-Spiritual Research
P.O. Box 741137
Arvada, CO 80006-1137
Tel/Fax 303-427-5311